T0045703

LIFE
CHANGING
LOVE

Resources by John Ortberg

An Ordinary Day with Jesus
(curriculum series, with Ruth Haley Barton)

Everybody's Normal Till You Get to Know Them
(book, ebook, audio)

God Is Closer Than You Think
(book, ebook, audio, curriculum with Stephen and Amanda Sorenson)

*If You Want to Walk on Water,
You've Got to Get Out of the Boat*
(book, ebook, audio, curriculum with Stephen and Amanda Sorenson)

Know Doubt
(book, ebook, formerly entitled *Faith and Doubt*)

Life-Changing Love
(book, ebook, audio)

The Life You've Always Wanted
(book, ebook, audio, curriculum with Stephen and Amanda Sorenson)

Living the God Life

The Me I Want to Be
(book, ebook, audio, curriculum with Scott Rubin)

Old Testament Challenge
(curriculum series, with Kevin and Sherry Harney)

Soul Keeping
(book, ebook, audio, curriculum with Christine M. Anderson)

When the Game Is Over, It All Goes Back in the Box
(book, ebook, audio, curriculum with Stephen and Amanda Sorenson)

Who Is This Man?
(book, ebook, audio, curriculum with Christine M. Anderson)

BESTSELLING AUTHOR

JOHN ORTBERG

LIFE
CHANGING
LOVE

MOVING GOD'S LOVE FROM
YOUR HEAD TO YOUR HEART

Previously titled *Love Beyond Reason*

ZONDERVAN

Life-Changing Love
Formerly *Love Beyond Reason*
Copyright © 1998 by John Ortberg

This title is also available as a Zondervan ebook.
Visit www.zondervan.com/ebooks.

This title is also available in a Zondervan audio edition.
Visit www.zondervan.fm.

Requests for information should be addressed to:
Zondervan, 3900 *Sparks Dr. SE, Grand Rapids, Michigan* 49546

This edition: ISBN 978-0-310-34208-3 (softcover)

Library of Congress Cataloging-in-Publication Data

Ortberg, John.
        Love beyond reason : moving God's love from your head to your heart / John
Ortberg.
            p. cm.
        Includes bibliographical references.
        ISBN 978-0-310-23449-4 (softcover)
        1. Love — Religious aspects — Christianity. 2. God — love. 3. God — Worship and
love. 4. Christian life. I. Title.
BV4639.O78 1998
231'.6 — dc21   98-26062

All Scripture quotations, unless otherwise indicated, are from the *New Revised Standard
Version,* copyright © 1989 by the Division of Christian Education of the National Council
of the Churches of Christ in the United States of America. Used by permission of
Zondervan. All rights reserved.

Scripture quotations marked NIV are taken from The Holy Bible, *New International
Version®, NIV®.* Copyright © 1973, 1978, 1984, 2011 by Biblica, Inc.® Used by permission. All
rights reserved worldwide.

All rights reserved. No part of this publication may be reproduced, stored in a retrieval
system, or transmitted in any form or by any means — electronic, mechanical, photocopy,
recording, or any other — except for brief quotations in printed reviews, without the prior
permission of the publisher.

Interior design: Sherri L. Hoffman

First printing March 2015 / Printed in the United States of America

To
Ian Pitt-Watson,
David Hubbard,
Lew Smedes, and
Rich Mouw
this book is gratefully dedicated

CONTENTS

ACKNOWLEDGMENTS

IAN PITT-WATSON WAS THE first preacher I'd ever heard who was also a poet, an artist. When listening to other preachers I often felt informed, convicted, or inspired. When listening to Ian it was sometimes as if a veil had parted, and I suddenly wasn't sure if I was sitting in a classroom in Pasadena or in first-century Jerusalem. To listen to Ian preach was often to find yourself suddenly, mysteriously, hopelessly immersed in the presence of God — to your own surprise most of all. Two of the great gifts of my life were the gifts first of his teaching, then of his friendship.

Maybe his greatest sermon was the story of two kinds of love — the love that seeks value in its object, and the love that creates value. Ian never published it, except a few bits to illustrate the craft of preaching. But it provides the central idea for the first chapter, the metaphor of a rag doll. The stories and experiences I tell in the first chapter are my own. Pandy really exists and is doing quite well in San Diego. But the inspiration came from Ian.

I also want to thank several people who read parts or all of this manuscript: Ruth Haley Barton, Gerald Hawthorne, Rich Mouw, Lauri Pederson, Scott Pederson, Lew Smedes, and Jodi Walli. Jack Kuhatschek was again a great help and friend as an editor, and Jim Ruark's diligent efforts added clarity where it was sorely needed.

To my wife, Nancy, for her candor and encouragement, and to Laura, Mallory, and Johnny, I owe the unpayable debt of all those who are loved despite their raggedness.

ONE

LOVE BEYOND REASON

Love slays what we have been that we may be what we were not.

ST. AUGUSTINE

HER NAME WAS PANDY. She had lost a good deal of her hair, one of her arms was missing, and, generally speaking, she'd had the stuffing knocked out of her. She was my sister Barbie's favorite doll.

She hadn't always looked like this. She had been a personally selected Christmas gift by a cherished aunt who had traveled to a great department store in faraway Chicago to find her. Her face and hands were made of some kind of rubber or plastic so that they looked real, but her body was stuffed with rags to feel soft and squeezable, like a real baby. When my aunt looked in the display window at Marshall Fields and found Pandy, she knew she had found something very good.

When Pandy was young and a looker, Barbie loved her. She loved her with a love that was too strong for Pandy's own good. When Barbie went to bed at night, Pandy lay next to her. When Barbie had lunch, Pandy ate beside her at the table. When Barbie could get away with it, Pandy took a bath with her. Barbie's love for that doll was, from Pandy's point of view, pretty nearly a fatal attraction.

By the time I knew Pandy, she was not a particularly attractive doll. In fact, to tell the truth she was a mess. She was no longer a very valuable doll; I'm not sure we could have given her away.

But for reasons that no one could ever quite figure out, in the way that kids sometimes do, my sister Barbie loved that little rag doll still. She loved her as strongly in the days of Pandy's raggedness as she ever had in her days of great beauty.

Other dolls came and went. Pandy was family. Love Barbie, love her rag doll. It was a package deal.

Once we took a vacation from our home in Rockford, Illinois, to Canada. We had returned almost all the way home when we realized at the Illinois border that Pandy had not come back with us. She had remained behind at the hotel in Canada.

No other option was thinkable. My father turned the car around and we drove from Illinois all the way back to Canada. We were a devoted family. Not a particularly bright family, perhaps, but devoted.

We rushed into the hotel and checked with the desk clerk in the lobby — no Pandy. We ran back up to our room — no Pandy. We ran downstairs and found the laundry room — Pandy was there, wrapped up in the sheets, about to be washed to death.

The measure of my sister's love for that doll was that she would travel all the way to a distant country to save her.

The years passed, and my sister grew up. She outgrew Pandy. She traded her in for a boyfriend named Andy (who, oddly enough, was even less attractive than the doll Pandy).

Pandy had not been much of a bargain for a long while, and by now the only logical thing left to do was to toss her out. But this my mother could not bring herself to do. She held Pandy one last time, wrapped her with exquisite care in some tissue, placed her in a box, and stored her in the attic for twenty years.

When I was growing up I had all kinds of casual playthings and stuffed animals. My mother didn't save any of them. But she saved Pandy. Want to guess why? (When I was younger I thought it was perhaps because my mother loved my bratty little sister more than she loved me.)

The nature of my sister's love is what made Pandy so valuable. Barbie loved that little doll with the kind of love that made the doll precious to anyone who loved Barbie. All those tears and hugs and secrets got mixed in with the rags somehow. If you loved Barbie, you just naturally loved Pandy too.

More years passed. My sister got married (not to Andy) and moved far away. She had three children, the last of whom was a little girl named Courtney, who soon reached the age where *she* wanted a doll.

No other option was thinkable. Barbie went back to Rockford, back to the attic, and dragged out the box. By this time, though, Pandy was more rag than doll.

So my sister took her to a doll hospital in California (there really is such a place) and had her go through reconstructive surgery. Pandy was given a facelift or liposuction or whatever it is that they do for dolls, until after thirty years Pandy became once again as beautiful on the outside as she had always been in the eyes of the one who loved her. I'm not sure she looked any better to Barbie, but now it was possible for others to view what Barbie had always seen in her.

When Pandy was young, Barbie loved her. She celebrated her beauty. When Pandy was old and ragged, Barbie loved her still. Now she did not simply love Pandy *because* Pandy was beautiful, she loved her with a kind of love that *made* Pandy beautiful.

More years passed. My sister's nest will soon be emptied. Courtney is a teenager now, preparing for young womanhood; Andy Jr. is already on the phone.

And Pandy? Pandy's getting ready for another box.

TWO TRUTHS

THERE ARE TWO TRUTHS about human beings that matter deeply. *We are all of us rag dolls.* Flawed and wounded, broken and bent. Ever since the Fall, every member of the human race has lived on the ragged edge. Partly our raggedness is something that happens *to* us. Our genes may set us up for certain weaknesses. Our parents may let us down when we need them most. But that's not the whole story. We each make our own deposits into the ragged account of the human race. We choose to deceive when the truth begs to be spoken. We grumble when a little generous praise is called for. We deliberately betray when we're bound by oaths of loyalty.

> *We are all of us rag dolls. Flawed and wounded, broken and bent.*

Like a splash of ink in a glass of water, this raggedness permeates our whole being. Our words and thoughts are never entirely free of it. We are rag dolls, all right.

But we are God's rag dolls. He knows all about our raggedness, and he loves us anyhow. Our raggedness is no longer the most important thing about us.

We were not created ragged. From the beginning there was a wonder about human beings that caused God himself to say "Very Good" as he looked at them in the department store window. There was a wonder about human beings that caused the writer of Genesis to say they had been made in God's own image. There was a wonder about human beings that caused the psalmist to say they rival the divine beings in glory and honor. There is a wonder about human beings still that even all our fallenness cannot utterly erase.

There is a wonder about you. Raggedness is not your identity. Raggedness is not your destiny, nor is it mine. We may be unlovely, yet we are not unloved.

And we cannot be loved without being changed. When people experience love (and here I don't mean simply having warm feelings toward others, I mean love that is sometimes stern and challenging and may even be painful), they begin to grow lovely.

This is true even at the physical level. Psychologists tell us that the excitement of being in love increases your heart rate: your face glows, your lips look more red, and under-eye circles actually become less noticeable! Heightened emotions cause your pupils to dilate, so that your eyes look brighter and clearer. We have been so constructed that even our bodies become lovelier when they are loved.

> We may be unlovely, yet we are not unloved.

We are most used to a type of love that looks for someone or something of great worth. This is a love that celebrates the beauty or strength of the beloved. The love we're most familiar with is drawn to an object because it is expensive or attractive or lends status to the one associated with it.

The Greeks had a ready word for this kind of love. It was the word *eros*. When we hear this word we may think of the term "erotic," but *eros* was about more than just sexual love. At its core, *eros* described that kind of love I give to what satisfies my desires, wins my admiration, or fulfills my appetites. *Eros* is love on a treasure hunt. It is the reward that goes along with winning the Miss America pageant; or being named *People* magazine's sexiest man of the year.

We learn about this kind of love early on. Studies show that adults smile at, coo over, kiss, and hold pretty babies more than plain ones. Fathers are more involved with attractive babies than those judged unattractive by independent raters.

Karen Lee-Thorp notes that children's stories reinforce this: "The prince was not enraptured with Cinderella's intelligent, sensitive conversation; he was smitten by her wardrobe and her teeny tiny feet. Snow White and Sleeping Beauty netted their men while comatose." Rapunzel spent twenty years alone in a tower and never had a bad hair day.

Eros — love that grows out of need and admiration and desire — is not necessarily a bad kind of love. It's good that a baby loves the mother whose milk means life. It's good for a lover to celebrate the beauty of his beloved.

But *eros* alone is too precarious a love to build your life on when you're a rag doll. You will be trapped in an unwinnable contest to prove you're pretty enough, smart enough, strong enough, or spiritual enough to deserve loving. You will be afraid to let the ragged edges of your true self show. No, rag dolls need love made of sterner stuff than mere *eros*.

There is such a love, a love that *creates* value in what is loved. There is a love that turns rag dolls into priceless treasures. There is a love that fastens itself onto ragged little creatures, for reasons that no one could ever quite figure out, and makes them precious and valued beyond calculation. This is a love beyond reason. This is the love of God. This is the love with which God loves you and me.

Love is why God created us in the first place. Theologians speak of the fact that God created everything freely, not out of necessity. This is a very important idea — it means that God did not make us because he was bored, lonely, or had run out of things to do.

God did not create us out of need. He created us out of his love. C. S. Lewis wrote, "God, who needs nothing, loves into existence wholly superfluous creatures in order that He may love and perfect them."

But the full extent of God's love was shown not so much when he chose to create us. It was shown when we had become sinful and unlovely.

Paul put it like this: "While we were still weak, at the right time Christ died for the ungodly. Indeed, rarely will anyone die for a righteous person — though perhaps for a good person someone might actually dare to die. But God proves his love for us in that while we still were sinners Christ died for us."

For God is fully aware of our secret. He knows that we are rag dolls. The prophet Isaiah said it thousands of years ago: "All of us have become like one who is unclean, and all our righteous acts are like filthy rags." Every one of us has become ragged, so damaged by sin and guilt that it seemed like the logical thing left was to discard the human race. Toss it out and start over.

But this God could not bring himself to do. So God proposed reconstructive surgery. God proposed to take the human race to where he could change filthy rags and remove the guilt and sin that left the objects of his love so unlovely.

There really is such a place. It is called the cross.

Normal human love might sometimes make sacrifices for a noble person, Paul says. But God has gone to the ultimate length to prove his love for us. He died for us at the *right time* — when we were ragged, weak, sinful.

The writers of Scripture didn't want to use the word *eros* to describe this kind of love. So for the most part they chose a fairly colorless word, the word *agape*. It hadn't been used much by the Greeks, but now it was filled with new meaning. It was used to describe the kind of love that could give hope to a rag doll.

The old English word for this kind of love is *charity*. Charity was used to express love in the form of pure gift. It's not used much anymore, and when it is, it often carries overtones that are patronizing or condescending. No one wants to be a "charity case."

But in the final run the ultimate love comes to us as a gift.

C. S. Lewis wrote:

> We are all receiving Charity. There is something in each of us that cannot be naturally loved. It is no one's fault if they do not so love it. Only the lovable can be naturally loved. You might as well ask people to like the taste of rotten bread or the sound of a mechanical drill. We can be forgiven, and pitied, and loved in spite of it, with Charity; no other way. All who have good parents, wives, husbands, or children may be sure that at some times they are receiving Charity, are not loved because they are lovable but because Love Himself is in those who love them.

CALLED TO LOVE

THERE ARE IN THE NEW TESTAMENT two commands that form the heart of our response to God's love. They cannot be separated. The whole of God's will comes down to this, Jesus said, "Love the Lord your God with all your heart, soul, mind and strength; and Love your neighbor as yourself." The primary form that loving God takes in the Bible is loving the people who mean so much to him. In the words of Jesus: "Whatever you did for the least of these, you did for me."

"Love me, love my rag dolls," God says. It's a package deal.

If we are serious about loving God, we must begin with people, all people. And especially we must learn to love those that the world generally discards.

In Jesus' day, it was the people who were most aware of their raggedness who were most open to his love. Jesus was eating one day at the home of a Pharisee named Simon, who felt, all things considered and even from God's point of view, that he really was not a difficult person to love.

A woman entered the house. Luke tells us she was "a sinner," which is most likely a polite way of saying she was a hooker. No doubt she was an uninvited guest, scandalizing everyone there except for the one truly holy person at the table. She had lost her reputation, a good deal of her virtue was missing, and generally speaking she'd had the stuffing knocked out of her. Her name was Pandy.

She hadn't always looked like this. There was a day when she had been someone's little girl, when someone cherished dreams for her, perhaps. When she had dreams herself, maybe. But that day had been gone a long time. It had been years since she had been in the public company of anyone respectable. It took all the courage she had to brave the looks and whispers in that room.

She stood behind Jesus, at his feet (people reclined rather than sat at a table in those days). But when she could bring herself to look into Jesus' eyes, rather than contempt she saw love.

She had brought perfume to anoint Jesus. This was generally done by pouring the perfume on the person's head. But as she watched Jesus, the tears came. Maybe she was thinking of how she earned the money to buy the perfume. Maybe she was thinking of the little girl she once was. Maybe she was thinking of the gap between who she had become and who she wanted to be. At any rate, instead of his head, she began to anoint Jesus' feet with a mixture of perfume and tears.

Then she did something — she let down her hair. This was never done. It was a violation of social custom; respectable Jewish women always kept their hair bound in public. As a prostitute, she had let down her hair

> Jesus is scandalously ready to forgive.

many times before. And each time was another wound to her heart, another scar on her soul. But this time it was for an act of homage, to dry the feet she had bathed and anointed. She who had let down her hair so many times before let it down once more. But this was the last time. This time she got it right. The days of her raggedness were about to end.

Simon waited for Jesus to point out who this woman was. Before we get too harsh with Simon, it's worth asking how *I* would have responded in his place. This woman had, after all, defied God with her life. She had lowered the standards of fidelity; she had helped wreck some homes, perhaps. It does no good to gloss over her raggedness. A word in favor of morality wouldn't seem out of place here.

But Jesus is scandalously ready to forgive. He understands as Simon does not that when there is authentic repentance the work of judgment has already been done. He points out to Simon that where Simon had neglected to provide water for Jesus' feet, she had bathed them with all that she had, mingled with tears. Where Simon had not offered him a kiss, she could not stop kissing his feet. Where Simon had not offered even inexpensive olive oil for his refreshment, she had anointed him with expensive perfume.

Simon could not receive much love, because he clung stubbornly to the notion that he did not need much forgiveness. His very sense of moral and spiritual superiority had caused him to lose a sense of his own raggedness. And so his heart had become even more unloving and unlovely than the sinner he despised.

But she knew. The woman knew all about who she was, and she knew that Jesus knew all about her and loved her anyway. And so she was transformed. "Your sins are forgiven. Your faith has saved you; go in peace," Jesus said to her, astonishing Simon even more than his guests, and the woman more than Simon.

"She may be a rag doll," Jesus said, "but she's my rag doll. Love me, love my rag dolls." It's a package deal.

What does this miracle of love consist of? Three things, I think, form the irreducible core of what love does. And I must learn to receive each of these elements of love from God if I am to flourish as his child.

Love Means Being *for* the One Who Is Loved

If I love someone, it means I have certain hopes and intentions and wishes for them. I'm in their corner. I long for them to flourish and blossom. I want them to realize all their potential. I want them to become filled with virtue and moral beauty. Love desires "that you may become blameless and pure, children of God without fault in a crooked and depraved generation, in which you shine like stars in the universe. . . ."

This means sometimes I may need to do that which will cause pain for the one I love. Love is often confused with softness. When we speak of doing "the loving thing," we sometimes think it means "always doing what the person I love would want me to do." This of course is not love; it's not even sane. Try it with a three-year-old, and odds are she'll never make it to four.

To say Jesus loves people is *not* to say he'll always do what they want him to do. Dan Allender writes: "If Christ had practiced the kind of love we advocate nowadays, he would have lived to a ripe old age." He goes on to say that in many cases authentic love "will unnerve, offend, disturb, or even hurt those who are being loved."

Being *for* someone is deeper than just wanting to spare them pain. If I am really *for* a person, I am willing to risk saying painful things, if pain is the only way to bring growth. "For the Lord disciplines those whom he loves." True love is ready to warn, reprove, confront, or admonish when necessary.

We are told that we should love each other as Christ loved the church and gave himself up for her so as "to present the church to himself in splendor, without a spot or wrinkle or anything of the kind — yes, so that she may be holy and without blemish." Notice Paul doesn't say Jesus loved the church "and said her spots and blemishes didn't matter." His plan is not just for a fifty-percent blemish reduction. Love longs for the other to enter into the splendor God intended — no spots, no wrinkles, no blemishes. Removing spots and blemishes is almost never pain-free. Sometimes, love means getting in someone's face and on someone's back.

> True love is ready to warn, reprove, confront, or admonish when necessary.

But only humbly, reluctantly. True love never *desires* to inflict pain for pain's sake. All too often I'm not only willing to inflict pain on someone, I'm looking forward to it. Probably a safe guideline is, I need to be very careful of creating pain for another person if I feel a twinge of enjoyment in the process. God's love moves him to bear infinitely more pain for our sakes than we ever could: "and sent his Son to be the atoning sacrifice for our sins."

To be *for* someone means I identify with him, I'm cheering him on; I celebrate her victories and mourn her setbacks. It means I deeply and sincerely wish him well.

This shows how difficult it is to love. It doesn't take much truth-telling for me to admit I don't want my enemies to succeed. More humbling is the fact that deep down I often don't even want my friends to succeed too much.

This is the truth that staggered the apostle Paul: for all his raggedness, God was *for* him: "If God is *for* us, who is against us? . . . Who will separate us from the love of Christ?"

To say that God loves us, then, means that God is *for* us. God longs for us to blossom and flourish beyond our own longings for ourselves.

Love Delights in and Enjoys the One Who Is Loved

This facet has to do with the heart of the one who loves. When I love you, it is not something I do simply out of duty or obligation.

I remember hearing a Christian speaker say that you should always love your spouse with an *in spite of* love, never with a *because of* love — but who wants to be on the receiving end of that? If, when I was proposing to my wife, I had said, "Well, there's certainly nothing about *you* that any reasonable person could ever warm up to, but because of my noble character I will hold my nose and love you anyway" the proposing process would not have gone nearly as well as it actually did.

No, when we love someone the mere sight of them causes our eyes to light up. This is beautifully expressed in Exodus at the burning bush when God tells Moses his brother Aaron is on his way: "Even now he is coming out to meet you, and when he sees you *his heart will be glad*." When you see someone you love, it makes your heart glad.

Love insists that the one loved *ought* to be loved. Love celebrates the beloved. This is why love has always been and always will be expressed most deeply in love *songs*.

It is very important to remember that God loves us in this way. Some Christian writers have written as if God loves us only *in spite of* ourselves. Of course, there is plenty God has to love us "in spite of." But raggedness is not the whole story about you. As Lewis Smedes put it, it may be a very bad thing that I needed God to die for me, but it is a wonderful thing that God thinks I'm worth dying *for*. We may be ragged, but we must never confuse raggedness with worthlessness.

> As Lewis Smedes put it, it may be a very bad thing that I needed God to die for me, but it is a wonderful thing that God thinks I'm worth dying for.

God doesn't just love you because he has to, he loves you because he wants to. God delights in you. Of course, that doesn't mean God delights in everything you do. Your own mother doesn't do that, if she's at all healthy. But the fact that you exist — *you, your own self* — is very good in God's eyes. God likes to love you.

The psalmist speaks of God watching him "as the apple of the eye." This little phrase "apple of your eye" is used a number of times in Scripture. It could be translated "the little man of the eye," or "the daughter of the eye." It's based on what happens when you look a person in the eye at point-blank range. You see an image of yourself in the eye of the other person. Apply this to your relationship with God: You will see yourself reflected in the gaze of the Father. You are the apple of God's eye.

Of course, all lovers are sometimes disappointed in those they love. They know the pain of unrequited love. Lovers don't just sing love songs; lovers more than all others sing the blues.

God too. "When Israel was a child, I loved him, and out of Egypt I called my son. The more I called them, the more they went from me. . . . it was I who taught Ephraim how to walk, I took them up in my arms; but they did not know that I healed them. I led them with cords of human kindness, with bands of love. . . . I bent down to them and fed them. . . . My people are bent on turning away from me."

God has supremely what all those who love share to some degree, what Charles Williams called the gift of double vision: ". . . all the worship under heaven ought not to prevent her lover from knowing [with reasonable accuracy and unreasonable love] when she is lazy, lewd, or malicious. She has a double nature, and he can have double sight." God sees with utter clarity who we are. He is undeceived as to our warts and wickedness. But when God looks at us that is not all he sees. He also sees who we are intended to be, who we will one day become. We sometimes say love is blind, but it is not so. Love alone truly sees, sees with this double vision. And in the act of seeing, God begins to call to the surface the goodness and beauty in us that is now visible only to him, so that one day it will be visible to all. And that makes his heart glad.

Love Gives to and Serves the One Loved

Most of all, love gives. Giving is to love what eating is to hunger. Giving is how love expresses itself. "God so loved the world that he *gave* . . ." begins the most familiar statement in Scripture.

Giving is love with character. Without acts of servanthood, love has no skeletal structure, nothing to support itself.

Eros finds giving easy in the early stages. Cards and flowers and foot rubs flow effortlessly as the Nile. The early rush of feelings supports this. These feelings are a kind of emotional training wheels, but sooner or later they have to come off. *Eros* may give, but only when it expects a fair rate of exchange.

The test of love is that it gives even when there is no expectation of a return.

Anne Lamott wrote of an eight-year-old boy who had a younger sister dying of leukemia. He was told that without a blood transfusion she would die. His parents asked if they could test his blood to see if it was compatible with hers. He said sure. They tested, and it was a match. Then they asked if he would give his sister a pint of his own blood, that it could be her only chance of living. He said he would have to think about it overnight.

The next day he told his parents he was willing to donate the blood. They took him to the hospital; he was put on a gurney beside his six-year-old sister. Both were hooked up to IVs. A nurse took a pint of blood from the boy, which was given to his sister. The boy lay in silence as the blood that would save his sister dripped from the IV, until the doctor came over to see how he was doing. Then the boy opened his eyes and asked, "How soon until I start to die?"

Love is never so fully love as when it gives.

One more story about a rag doll. This one's name is Al.

Al was my father-in-law. He was an uncomplicated man, easy to like. He was a natural athlete and avid outdoorsman who loved to hunt and fish. When we had a

> The test of love is that it gives even when there is no expectation of a return.

daughter (his first grandchild; my wife has no siblings) we didn't realize how excited Al was about the prospect of taking her to the Great Outdoors with him. Until one day we were driving home from their house, where Laura had been secretly coached by Al for some time. She was a year old, and we were putting her through one of the routines that all firstborns have to endure:

"Laura, what sound does a kitty make?"

"Meow."

"And what sound does a doggie make?"

"Woof, woof."

"And what sound does a birdie make?"

"BANG!"

Her grandfather wanted her to know.

Al was the kind of man who didn't mind what might get said about his wife or daughter, but he never tolerated an insult to his dog. Eppie was (to tell the truth) sadly obese by the time I knew her, but Al would never hear of it. He insisted she was a special breed — a "short-legged Lab" — and the reason her stomach was so close to the ground was not because it was so large but because her legs were too short to provide much clearance.

Al's ragged edge ran toward the bottle. He was an alcoholic, as were his father, uncle, and brother. Not the sloppy kind, he didn't miss work or throw away money, but it made him hard to get to know. Nancy always knew her dad loved her, but it was in his own way, a ragged way. He never said it outright. Sometimes if she told him she loved him, over the phone, he might say, "Me too, punk," but he never volunteered it.

One fall his skin turned yellow — the shade of an overripe banana — and the doctors told him they wanted to test him for pancreatic cancer, which at the time was virtually always terminal. We were waiting at his house for him to come home with the test results. "Got it!" were his first words when he came in the door. He didn't say much more about it. Sometimes we would see him staring out the window, but it was hard to know what he was thinking.

He had never been very concerned about God one way or the other. He wasn't particularly hostile, just casually disinterested. We tried to talk with him now but didn't get far.

Until one day when my mother was visiting. She talked to Al about how they shared the same grandchildren, about how life was unpredictable — maybe she would go first — but if Al should die, and the grandkids should ask someday about him and God, what should she tell them? How did it stand between Al and God?

"Fine," he said. "Everything's fine with God and me. Why shouldn't it be?"

She pressed further and explained about how "God proves his love for us in that while we still were sinners Christ died for us."

The light dawned, the ice melted, and Al prayed and gave his life to God.

And God began some reconstructive surgery. Al and I began to read together from the gospel of John. He would study some on his own, then we'd talk about it, and generally pray after. Once or twice we even prayed holding hands.

One day when the cancer was quite advanced Al was lying in our bed, too weak and emaciated to sit up, and we'd finished talking about Jesus.

"Now let's pray," Al said, which was striking because he hadn't often initiated prayer before.

"Okay."

"And let's do that hand thing," Al said. He reached over and grabbed my hand.

And it struck me that the hand that had spent a lifetime throwing footballs and swinging golf clubs and casting and shooting and lifting countless cans of beer was more beautiful in weakness than it had ever been in its strength.

Not long after that Al went into the hospital. On a Friday night, he called for Nancy. They talked for a while, then before Nancy hung up the phone I heard her say one of the few phrases that I will remember as long as I live.

"I love you *too*, Dad," she said.

I asked her if that meant what I thought it did.

Yes, her dad said he loved her.

That was on a Friday night. The next morning, Al suffered a stroke, which is not uncommon given his condition and treatment. For six weeks he was virtually unable to speak or control the simplest of bodily functions, and then he died.

The last time Nancy heard her dad speak was the first time he said, "I love you."

There is a kind of love that seeks value in that which is loved. There is a kind of love that is attracted to status and wealth and beauty. We understand that love. We see it every day.

But there is a kind of love that creates value in that which is loved. There is a love that takes rag dolls like Al and you and me and loves us beyond all reason. And if you let him, God will begin to do reconstructive surgery on you, until one day — watch out! "See what love the Father has given us, that we should be called children of God; and that is what we are. . . . Beloved, we are God's children now; what we will be has not yet been revealed."

"Love me, love my rag dolls," God says. It's a package deal.

Two

LOVE PAYS ATTENTION

[God] crowds upon us from Sheol to the sea; he jostles our thoughts along the pathways in our brains. He hides in the bushes, jumping out in flames to startle us into seeing. He sequesters himself in stables and swaddling so as to take us unawares. He veils himself in flesh, the same flesh that drips into fingers at the end of my arms and sprouts into hair on my head.

VIRGINIA STEM OWENS

It is a common scene. A couple sits at the breakfast table. One spouse (let's say the husband) is immersed in the newspaper, while the wife is pouring out her heart. Frustrated, she finally complains, "You're not listening to me."

"I can repeat every word you've said," is the standard response. He proceeds to demonstrate. Is she satisfied? No! She doesn't want him simply to be able to replay her words — a tape recorder could do that. She wants him to be fully present. She wants him to put down the paper, look her in the eye, and pay attention to her.

Being heard is not enough. She wants to be attended to.

THE POWER OF ATTENTION

Attention is one of the most powerful forces in the world. Along with food and water, a baby needs the attentive gaze of a human face. A baby lies in the crib and smiles, the face smiles back, and the baby realizes that someone is watching, is responding, that what the baby does counts. The baby's joy or anger or sorrow is reflected in the face of another. Psychologists speak of this as *attunement*. The baby realizes it is possible to be somehow connected to — in tune with — another human being. The face scowls, perhaps, or disappears, and the baby tries to figure out what happened, how to bring it back. This face becomes the mirror through which the child learns whether it is a source of delight or disappointment. A child simply cannot survive without the face. The face is what tells the baby that it matters.

Erik Erikson writes, "Hardly has one learned to recognize the familiar face (the original harbor of basic trust) when he becomes also frightfully aware of the unfamiliar, the strange face, the unresponsive, the averted . . . and the frowning face. And here begins . . . that inexplicable tendency on man's part to feel that he has caused the face to turn away which happened to turn elsewhere."

> Being heard
> is not enough.
> She wants to
> be attended to.

When we grow up, we still need to be attended to. In one study, according to Gerald Egan, at a prearranged signal students switched from a slouched, passive, no-eye-contact posture to leaning forward and looking attentively at the teacher. The teacher, who had been mumbling from his notes in a colorless monotone, gradually responded by beginning to gesture, look at the students, and speak at a faster and more energetic rate. At another signal the students switched back to their old style, and the teacher, "after some painful seeking for continued reinforcement," reverted to his old monotone.

There have been times in preaching when I've felt like whole congregations are secretly in on that experiment. Every speaker knows that when you speak, there are certain people that encourage you, that feed you, just by paying attention. There are certain faces you look for because, by their look or smile or nod, they are saying, *Keep going! What you say matters. Proclaim the truth!*

One of the great miracles of life is that God pays attention to us. This is partly why the writers of Scripture speak so often of God's face. This is the hope of the great priestly blessing that God himself taught the people of Israel:

> The LORD bless you and keep you;
> the LORD make his face shine upon you
>   and be gracious to you;
> the LORD turn his face toward you
>   and give you peace.

To turn your face toward someone is to give that person your whole-hearted, undivided attention. It is not the casual listening of a preoccupied mind. It is a statement: "I have nothing else to do, nowhere I'd rather be. I'm fully devoted to being with you." This is the kind of attention God lavishes on us.

It gets better. This blessing says God will not only turn his face toward us, he will make it "shine" on us. The shining face is an image of delight. It is the face of a proud parent beaming while a child plays in her first piano recital. It is the radiant face of a bride as she walks the aisle to her groom. We can turn our face toward (pay attention to) anyone, with a little effort. But our faces shine and beam and grow radiant only in the presence of those we love most deeply. And this, says the prayer, is how God loves us. God pays attention to us.

In contrast, to lose God's loving attention was, to the psalmist, to lose everything:

> "Come," my heart says, "seek his face!"
> Your face, LORD, do I seek.
> Do not hide your face from me.
> Do not turn your servant away in anger,
> you who have been my help.
> Do not cast me off, do not forsake me,
> O God of my salvation!

Nothing was worse to the psalmist than the thought of God's "hiding his face."

Attention is so valuable we don't just *give* it, we *pay* attention. It's like money. And, like money, it generally flows to those who have status. The more important you are, the more people will pay attention to what you say. In *Fiddler on the Roof*, Tevye the milkman muses that if he were rich, all the village movers and shakers would hang on his every word — even if he didn't have a clue what he was talking about. "When you're rich, they think you really know."

> This is how
> God loves us.
> God pays
> attention to us.

The gospel of John tells the story of a man who certainly had no worldly riches and whom no one paid attention to. He had spent his entire life being ignored. He was simply not worth noticing. He was blind; he was a beggar.

To get to where I used to work I often drove through an intersection where I saw a certain man dressed in old army fatigues, standing by the road, holding up a sign: "Will work for food." In most cases, those of us waiting for the light to change would avert our eyes. Sometimes I would give him a dollar, more often I'd pretend not to notice him.

That was the life of the man John wrote about. People would try to look the other way; he would try to do something to catch their attention. He was used to being ignored. It was what he did for a living. He was just another face in the crowd.

But not to Jesus.

The very first words in this story are that "as he walked along, he [Jesus] *saw* a man blind from birth." This is the first miracle in the story. Here is a man not only blind, but invisible. How many years had it been since another human being had turned his face on such a one? But Jesus, who, after all, had places to go and things to do ("as he walked along . . .") actually *looked* at him. Jesus saw the hurt and disappointment of a life lived in dependence and anonymity. Jesus saw the hopelessness of a life lived in endless night that would never know dawn.

No one has ever *seen* like Jesus.

Jesus noticed a tax collector sitting inconspicuously up in a sycamore tree. He felt it when a woman desperate for healing touched the hem of his robe, even though he was jostled by bustling crowds. He saw a widow no one else would have given a second glance and observed that she gave everything she had. She made his face shine. He gave recognition to unimportant little children that the crowd was trying to make disappear. His teachings all reflect this aspect of Jesus: he noticed the way mustard seeds grow and yeast spreads; the way people jockey for seats of honor at parties and high-status titles in their little communities. He noticed when his friends argued about who was the greatest disciple; he noticed their doubt and fear on a stormy boat ride; sometimes they wished he didn't notice quite so much.

No one has ever *seen* like Jesus.

All through this story various verbs meaning "to see" pop up. One who is pitied for his blindness will turn out to have true spiritual insight. Those who think of themselves as most insightful will turn out to be spiritually blind. But John starts the story with Jesus' act. Jesus *sees* a man everyone else has learned to ignore. *Love me, love my rag dolls,* Jesus says.

Living in God's love requires new eyes. We must learn to continually see God's grace at work all around us.

Jesus was the master of this. For him, it was simply apparent that we live in a God-bathed world. He could not open his eyes without seeing the signs. "Look at the birds," he'd tell his friends. They don't sow or reap or stow away in barns. They have no Day-Timers or strategic plans. They never get colitis or ulcers or high blood pressure. But our heavenly Father feeds them all the time. The Lover of Rag Dolls is at it again.

Every time you wake up, think a thought, enjoy a meal, your experiences are not random occurrences. They are gracious gifts from your Father.

The God of the Bible is the God who *notices*. "O LORD, you have searched me and known me," the psalmist says. There is not the smallest detail of your life that is not of immense interest to God.

Jesus was convinced of this. This is why he said, "Are not two sparrows sold for a penny? Yet not one of them will fall to the ground apart from your Father. And even the hairs of your head are all counted. So do not be afraid; you are of more value than many sparrows."

> Your experiences are not random occurrences. They are gracious gifts from your Father.

By the way, if you miss Jesus' wonderful playfulness in his last phrase, you miss the whole point. Jesus noticed how anxiety robs us of life: *Does anyone notice?* we wonder. *Does anyone care?* So he points out the Father's ceaseless attentiveness to sparrows — about the least expensive creature people might buy in his day. *So don't worry,* he gently teases. *You are worth quite a few sparrows.*

How many sparrows would it take to equal the value of your life in God's eyes? Put every sparrow that has ever flown on one side of the scales, you on the other, and God will take you every time. If God attends to every mishap in any moment of every sparrow's life, try to imagine how closely he attends to you.

In the story of the blind man, because Jesus pays attention to this man, the disciples notice him as well.

The disciples ask, "Who sinned, this man or his parents, that he was born blind?" This is a strange question — how could he have *caused* his own blindness if he were born with it?

There was a belief in those days that it was possible to be born guilty of specific sin. For instance, if a mother-to-be worshiped in a heathen temple, the unborn child was judged to be guilty of idolatry. One ancient writing referred to a baby born with a deformity because its mother walked through a pagan grove of trees and was "delighted." There was a school of thought that held it was possible for a fetus to sin.

Generally in those days people believed in a cause-and-effect relationship between suffering and sin. Somehow it made people feel better if they could think that a suffering person *deserved* his suffering. When we judge people, we feel less of an obligation to suffer with and for them. When we judge people, we cease to pay attention to them. People knew what category to put this man in: beggar, blind, sinner. Rag doll. They did not look beyond the labels to see the uniqueness of *this particular man*.

So this man spent his life being ignored. He was blind; people would find that depressing. He was a beggar; people would find that demanding. He was, in their minds, a product of sin, which meant they would find him disgusting.

Mothers would walk by with their children: "Don't look at him; don't listen to him; don't pay any attention to him. Pretend like you don't notice him. He is sinful. He wants something, and he doesn't deserve it."

Jesus comes to this man whom everyone else ignores, and he stops. His disciples want to know if the man had been cursed because of his own sin or that of his parents. They looked at the man, but they did not *see* what Jesus *saw*. They saw an object for an interesting theological discussion. Their seeing didn't draw them *to the man himself*. Whose fault is it — his or his parents'?

Jesus says, "You haven't been paying attention. God hasn't forsaken him. God has come to him." This is just the kind of person Jesus is looking for.

Ralph Ellison wrote of the pain of life as an African American in white society: "I am an invisible man. . . . I am a man of substance, of flesh and bone, fiber and liquids — and I might even be said to possess a mind. *I am invisible, understand, simply because people refuse to see me*."

Someone once asked Mother Teresa what she *saw* as she walked the streets of Calcutta where the poorest of the poor lived; what she saw when she looked at the orphans, the starving, the dying. This is what she said: "I see Jesus in a distressing disguise."

Notice when Jesus did this work of God: "as he walked along." John gives the story a very casual introduction. Jesus was traveling. He was not on the clock. He was not in a synagogue, not giving the Sermon on the Mount, not feeding 5,000. He was not in a formal ministry situation at all.

> What is the work of God? It is simply to see what Jesus would see if he were looking through my eyes, and respond as he would respond.

The main place you do the work of God is *as you go along.* It doesn't have to be in high-profile, important positions. It will happen, if it happens at all, in the routine, unspectacular corners of your life. *As you go along.*

This is your day. This is your opportunity to do the work of God. Don't miss it. If you do, you don't get it back. Night is coming. Don't miss the day.

What is the work of God? It is simply to see what Jesus would see if he were looking through my eyes, and respond as he would respond.

The religious leaders were blinded by their own spiritual sense of self-righteousness. *This man is not from God,* they said, *for he does not observe the Sabbath.*

Observing the Sabbath was one of the ways they distinguished themselves. Thirty-nine separate works were forbidden on the Sabbath, and most of these had sub-categories. You were not even allowed to cut your fingernails, pluck a hair from your head or your beard, or wear sandals with iron nails (sandals that had been woven together were allowed, but if they had nails in them each time you raised your foot it would count as bearing a burden).

One such forbidden act was making clay. You couldn't do any mixing or kneading — and this Jesus had done to make the clay that he put on the man's eyes.

Also, as a general practice, healing was not allowed on the Sabbath. The rule was, you could receive medical attention on the Sabbath only if your life was in actual danger. And even then it could only be for the purpose of keeping you from dying, not for *improving* your condition. They spelled out details: if your hand or foot was dislocated, you were not allowed to pour cold water over it, because cold water might help heal the sprain.

Ironically, part of the purpose of the Sabbath as it is commanded in Deuteronomy 5 was to focus attention on those most likely to be overlooked; its observance was to be extended to children and slaves and aliens so that all could have rest: "Remember that you were a slave in the land of Egypt . . . ," Moses said.

The Pharisees looked at this formerly blind man, but they did not see a reason to rejoice. They did not see the presence of the kingdom of God in their midst. They saw only a violated Sabbath. They saw a threat to a religious system that propped up their sense of their own spiritual superiority. They looked at the same man Jesus looked at, but *they did not see what Jesus saw*. They were too busy attending to their own status to pay attention to God.

They were so devoted to showing their righteousness that they missed the essence of the work of God, which is love. They did not see what Jesus saw, so they did not do what Jesus did.

John includes a detail that tells us just how ignored this man had been. After his healing he returned to his neighborhood: "The neighbors and those who had seen him before as a beggar began to ask, 'Is this not the man who used to sit and beg?' Some were saying, 'It is he.' Others were saying, 'No, but it is someone like him.' He kept saying, 'I am the man.' "

This man has been blind from birth. So he has been out begging, in the same place, for his whole life: perhaps thirty or forty years. These people — his neighbors, people who lived and worked where he begged — had been with him all that time. For thirty or forty years, day after day, he had been part of their world.

But they had paid so little attention to him that when the miracle happened they were not even able to identify him. They didn't even know what he looked like — some didn't even think he was the same man!

Meanwhile the Pharisees are so committed to undermining this man's credibility that they call his parents in for questioning: "Is this your son, who you say was born blind? How then does he now see?"

They respond: "We know that this is our son, and that he was born blind; but we do not know how it is that now he sees, nor do we know who opened his eyes. Ask him; he is of age. He will speak for himself."

Mom and Dad are not going terribly far out on a limb here to protect their boy. I'd like to think my folks would be a little more committed.

But John goes on to tell us they're afraid of being put out of the synagogue. As Lesslie Newbigin put it, "They are in the same world as the authorities — a world ruled by fear. They fear the authorities, and the 'authorities' fear for their 'authority.'"

So they call this man back in for a second round. Remember, this is a man who has spent his whole life being ignored. Now all of a sudden people are falling all over themselves to get at him. First Jesus and his disciples, then his neighbors, then he is dragged off to see the religious leaders. Now he's in for his second interview: they have a clear agenda, which is to get him to say something that will discredit Jesus. The way he handles himself is amazing. He is one of the most compelling characters in John's gospel:

"Give glory to God," they say, which is a high-pressure tactic for getting him to tell the truth as they want to hear it. "We know," they say, "we know this man is a sinner." What makes their blindness incurable is their claim of certainty. John keeps contrasting their closed-mindedness ("we know" they say three separate times) with the man's confessed ignorance ("I do not know" he says, three times). If only they would be open to the possibility that they *don't* know.

"I do not know whether he is a sinner," the formerly blind man says. "One thing I do know, that though I was blind, now I see."

"What did he do to you? How did he open your eyes?"

"I told you once, and you did not *pay attention.*" Then, with marvelous chutzpah, "Why do you want to hear it again? Do you also want to become his disciples?"

Now we begin to see the extent of their blindness. Here's the irony: they think of themselves as being totally devoted to the work of God. But they are so consumed with themselves that when God himself comes,

> They are so consumed with themselves that when God himself comes, they never notice.

they never notice. They are not paying attention. They fail to recognize the presence of the very God they claim to serve so faithfully. What other word than blind can you use to describe them?

LEARNING TO ATTEND TO GOD

THE FIRST WORK OF living in God's love is learning to pay attention to him.

> Listen, you that are deaf;
> and you that are blind, look up and see!
> Who is blind but my servant? . . .
> He sees many things, but does not observe them;
> his ears are open, but he does not hear.

God says even his own servant and his own people are afflicted with spiritual blindness. This means that we cannot naturally attend to God on our own. We will need to learn how.

William Barry and William Connolly write, "Our faith tells us that God communicates with us whether we know it or not by continuously creating and redeeming us. He shares himself with us even when we do not know that he is doing so. . . . We are being 'spoken to' continuously." But we cannot hear him because we do not know how to listen.

One afternoon my family waited in a sitting room for my sister to come up from her dorm to join us for Family Day. In the same room was a mother of a classmate of my sister, who was waiting with her eight-year-old son. For an hour and fifteen minutes we waited, and I don't suppose that woman stopped talking longer than it took to inhale. She talked — as the saying went before the day of compact discs — as if she'd been vaccinated with a phonograph needle. She talked as if words were the rope that kept her tethered to the earth. She talked until I knew more about her family than I did about some of my closest relatives.

Finally her daughter stepped into the room. "Well, we must be going," said the mom, keeping the torrent flowing. "I have to get reservations for dinner. We have to meet my husband at the restaurant, you know, and oh, yes, I need to stop by the store and get some buttons."

Then her son spoke. The only words, as best I can recollect it, that he uttered during the whole hour and fifteen minutes. He turned to his mother and said as only an eight-year-old could: "Mother, you need a button for your mouth."

Out of the mouths of babes.

All of us were thinking it, but only an eight-year-old had the nerve or honesty or foolishness to utter it. You need a button for your mouth.

I suspect that there are times when, if God had anything to say to me at all, it would be this: You need a button for your mouth.

"I am the God of the universe, maker of heaven and earth. I designed your body, I fashioned your world, I created your potential. I have wisdom and guidance and love that I long to communicate to you but I can't get through. Your heart and life are too noisy, and I will not scream. I love you. But you need a button for your mouth."

SPIRITUAL ATTENTION DEFICIT DISORDER

THE FIRST TASK IN spiritual life, the one to which we must return over and over, is simply this: to pay attention to God. This is challenging enough, considering the difficulty we have paying attention to anyone. Add to that the challenge of attending to a holy, mysterious, invisible God, and always our sin will attempt to distract us. We all have a kind of spiritual attention deficit disorder.

Basil Pennington uses the metaphor of a pond to describe the importance of stillness in paying attention to God. When you throw a stone into a pond, the stone will create ripples that reach to the shore all the way around — but only if the pond is still. When the pond is quiet and still, the arrival of the stone can be read over the entire surface.

But when the pond is not still, when the surface of the water is already ruffled and tossed, the arrival of the stone will go undetected. Where wind has disturbed the surface, the stone can't be disturbing. Where a storm is present, there is so much commotion already going on that no one will notice a few waves more or less. They will be lost in the frantic motion of the surface.

> Stillness is always the prerequisite for receptivity.

Stillness is always the prerequisite for receptivity. Telephones and television sets cannot receive messages when they are too filled with static and noise. Stillness first, then listening. The order cannot be reversed. "Be still, and know that I am God," quotes the psalmist.

One of the most powerful expressions of this is found in Psalm 131.

> O LORD, my heart is not lifted up,
> my eyes are not raised too high. . . .
> But I have calmed and quieted my soul,
> like a weaned child with its mother;
> my soul is like the weaned child that is with me.

An unweaned child is a noisy child. The unweaned child has learned that eventually noise leads to the satisfaction of its desires. Even if it doesn't, the noise itself appears to bring some relief. Or at least it makes others as miserable as the unweaned one.

The weaned child, however, has learned that the presence of the mother is about more than immediate gratification of desire. The weaned child has become capable of stillness. The weaned child can have a whole new form of communication with the mother. The weaned child has entered into a whole new relationship with its mother. Now the mother is more than simply one who exists to satisfy need, to take away hunger. The mother can become a person, not just a need-meeter.

There is a catch, of course. Weaning is not a popular process. At least, not for the "weanee." Children rarely volunteer for it because it is both costly and painful. Weaning means learning to live in stillness with unfulfilled desires. It is the mark of maturity.

The psalmist says this is a picture of my soul. I have learned to still my heart. There has been a spiritual weaning process so that I am no longer at the mercy of my desires and reflexes and demands. God is becoming more than just the Meeter of My Needs. I am entering into a new era of listening. I have stilled my soul.

How often is God at work, seeking to speak to me if only I'll listen?

- I am ready to speak in anger, to say hurtful words, but something gives me pause, and I find myself holding my tongue.
- I walk past the room of one of my children, moving quickly, but something prompts me to turn back and go inside just when they need someone to speak to.
- I am in a restaurant, being waited on but not noticing the server. Suddenly, for some reason, I am drawn to look — really *look* — at him. And then to talk with him. He is about my age, with children like mine. He does not speak English well. He has to work terribly hard for his family, at two jobs. I am

struck by how he needs prayer, and opportunities, and by how much I have been given and am responsible for.

Perhaps each of these moments is no accident. Perhaps in each of them God is whispering to me. Perhaps for every one of them that I notice, there are a thousand that pass by unobserved.

For my mind is not very stilled. It is disturbed by commotion that makes it very hard for me to discern the messages that come from God.

My mind is noisy with disordered desires. How do I appear to people? How successful will I be? What will I possess? How attractive am I?

My mind is disturbed by the static of anxiety that accompanies little faith: What will happen tomorrow? What if I run out of ideas? What if we don't have enough money? What if I can't solve some problem?

My mind is choppy from the turbulence of sin. Past regrets speak loudly to me of my spiritual inadequacy. Guilt shouts to me of my hypocrisy. Doublemindedness drives me forward one moment and backward the next.

Love notices.
Love listens.
Love remembers.

My mind loses its tranquillity due to sheer busyness. Too many commitments, too much activity, too little sleep, too much stimulation, too much talking — all these interfere with stillness and keep me from being able to discern the pebble, the "still small voice," that is the signal God wants to speak.

LEARNING TO ATTEND TO PEOPLE

IN ADDITION TO ATTENDING TO GOD, I am called to attend to the people who mean so much to him. The work of love is the work of paying attention. Love notices. Love listens. Love remembers. When is her birthday? What kind of coffee does he like? What is his favorite movie? Love is in the details. Deborah Tannen writes a wonderful story about a rag doll:

> My great-aunt, for many years a widow, had a love affair when she was in her seventies. Obese, balding, her hands and legs misshapen by arthritis, she did not fit the stereotype of a woman romantically loved. But she was — by a man, also in his seventies, who lived in a nursing home but occasionally spent weekends with her in her apartment. In trying to tell me what this relationship meant to her, my great-aunt told of a conversation. One evening she had had dinner out, with friends. When she returned home, her male friend called and she told him about the dinner. He listened with interest and asked her, "What did you wear?" When she told me this, she began to cry: "Do you know how many years it's been since anyone asked me what I wore?"
>
> When my great-aunt said this, she was saying that it had been years since anyone cared deeply — intimately — about her.

When I began graduate school, all of us aspiring psychologists were taught what was called SOLER posture. To communicate attentiveness to our clients, we were to Squarely face them, have Open posture (no crossed limbs), Lean toward them, maintain appropriate Eye contact, and stay Relaxed. The first time I met with a client I spent the first fifteen minutes concentrating so hard to maintain each element of the SOLER position that I didn't hear a word she said. I subsequently discovered that the best way to make someone feel attended to is to actually pay attention.

"Let everyone be quick to listen, slow to speak," said James, giving what might be the single most violated commandment in all Scripture.

If you want to do the work of God, pay attention to people. Notice them. Especially notice the people nobody else notices. When you pay attention to someone, when you focus totally on them, you say, "You are the most important thing in my world right now."

Love is a form of work. Scott Peck writes, "The principal form that the work of love takes is attention. When we love another person we give him or her our attention; we attend to that person's growth."

Dr. James Lynch, codirector of the Psychophysiological Clinic and Laboratories of the University of Maryland, has studied attention. He discovered that a genuine healing of the cardiovascular system takes place when we listen. Studies revealed that blood pressure rises when people speak and lowers when they listen.

> God notices things your mother has never even thought about.

God pays close attention to us: "Even the hairs of your head are numbered," Jesus said. We often take it as a sign of love if someone is able to notice a haircut or a change in hairstyle. (By the same token, the failure to notice a change in coiffure is one of the leading causes of conflict in marriage.)

God has numbered every hair. If one falls out, he notices. (He may not replace it, unfortunately, but he notices.) God notices things your mother has never even thought about. And when we live in the love of God, we begin to pay attention to people the way God pays attention to us.

In relating the story of the blind man, John wants his readers to know that Jesus has mastered the art of attending.

Each of the characters or groups of people in the story *saw* in a different way.

- When the disciples looked at this beggar, they saw an interesting theological conundrum — who sinned that he was born blind? But they did not see him with the eyes of the heart. Their seeing did not *move* them.

- When his neighbors looked at him, they saw an eyesore, a ragged reminder of suffering and poverty that they learned to overlook. But they did not see him with the eyes of the heart. They too were unmoved.
- When the Pharisees looked at him, they saw a violated Sabbath, a threat to their spiritual authority. They saw with dry, unblinking eyes — no tears, no softening. They did not simply *fail* to see, they *refused* to see. They tightly shut the eyes of the heart and would not open them. Spiritual blindness is not just ignorance. Jesus said to the Pharisees, "If you were blind, you would not have sin. But now that you say, 'We see,' your sin remains." Eyes that *cannot* see might be healed, but eyes that *will not* see cannot be helped. God himself will not force them open.

> Eyes that *cannot* see might be healed, but eyes that *will not* see cannot be helped.

- When Jesus looked at the blind man, Jesus saw an opportunity to do the work of God. He saw a child of God who needed to be delivered from blindness. He saw and was moved. He saw through eyes that sometimes glistened with tears, flashed with anger, or danced in joy. But they never missed a thing, those eyes.

And so a man who had been blind his whole life was given new eyes. Not just physically but spiritually. He began to see who Jesus was.

At first all the blind man knew was that his healer was the man they call Jesus (John 9:11). Later, to the Pharisees, he confessed this Jesus is a *prophet* (v. 17). Later still he became a defender of Jesus and said what Jesus has done shows he is *from God* (v. 33). By his final encounter, he had come to see Jesus as the *Son of Man*, and he bowed down to worship him (v. 38).

A man who had been blind from birth can see; and he realizes that the sight he will prize his whole life, the best thing he will ever lay his eyes on, is the One who healed him.

For now he sees that he has not been forgotten by God. Now he realizes, after a lifetime of being ignored, that God has not turned his face away from even the lowliest of rag dolls. God heard every prayer, counted every tear.

Now this man had eyes that could truly see. And I imagine he spent the rest of his life learning to see the way Jesus saw.

That's what eyes are for.

THREE

GOD TOUCHES THE
UNTOUCHABLE

*To love at all is to be vulnerable. Love anything, and your
heart will certainly be wrung, and possibly be broken. . . .
The only place outside Heaven where you can be perfectly safe
from all the dangers and perturbations of love is Hell.*

C. S. LEWIS

When I was growing up, the most dreaded childhood disease
was neither chicken pox, measles, nor mumps. It was a more
subtle and mysterious disorder. It was highly contagious. There
was no vaccine, no antidote, no inoculation.

No one ever elaborated what happened to you if you contracted this disease, but the mere mention of it struck terror in the
hearts of my friends and me. It was, we knew, a fate worse than
death. The only way to be safe was to place any carriers in strict
quarantine.

Fortunately, they were easily recognizable. The disease was
carried by girls. Every girl (except my mother) was loaded with
it. I'm not sure of the medical term, but we called it *cooties*. All a
carrier had to do was touch you, breathe on you, or look at you
real hard, and you'd be infected. Nobody was crazy enough to
touch someone with cooties. It was as if all carriers had a sign hung
from their necks: "Don't touch." If I'd have known then that I'd
end up in a house with three girls, I'd have gone crazy. I'm living
in cootiesville.

Human beings need to be touched. Gary Smalley and John Trent cite studies showing that people who experience meaningful touch on a regular basis actually have a longer life expectancy than those who don't. We naturally describe intimacy in spatial terms — being close to someone versus being distant. Psychologists have found that the greater the physical distance a couple maintains during conversation, the more likely they are to be dissatisfied with their marriage, and the more likely, ultimately, they are to get divorced.

Sometimes people are declared unfit to be touched. *The Economist* tells of an incident in the northern state of Bihar in India, in June of 1994, when a lower-caste girl eloped with an untouchable boy. With the approval of the village council, the boy's head was smashed in with a stone, while the girl was whipped and branded with a burning log. Such was the fate of the untouchable and one who would touch him.

Though the results are not always this dramatic, every society has its own untouchables, based on race, status, language, or education. And all of us, at certain stages or in certain settings, feel like untouchables — unacceptable, unworthy outsiders.

This is the story of a person who had been infected with a horrible disease; nobody would even go near him, let alone touch him. But then Somebody did. It is also the story about a world that has been infected with a horrible disease. But God touched it. It is your story and mine.

The man in this story had leprosy. Let me take a moment to describe this disease as it was understood in the first century. The most common kind began with a sense of lethargy and pain in the joints. Soon discolored patches and nodules left the face of the victim unrecognizable. When the sores ulcerated, the stench was intolerable. The vocal cords would also ulcerate, leaving the person's voice hoarse and raspy.

The great damage from leprosy came from a loss of sensation. Dr. Paul Brand has been a leading researcher of leprosy in the twentieth century, spending much of his career with lepers in India. He writes of trying to get into a padlocked gate, but the rusty lock wouldn't yield to his key. A young leper put his finger into the lock and twisted it until the lock opened. When he pulled his finger out, Brand saw it had been gnashed to the bone, but the boy couldn't feel it.

Lepers often lose fingers and toes, and people used to think this was caused by the disease. Brand and some of his researchers stayed up at night watching the lepers as they slept. Rats would come and gnaw at the lepers' extremities, but because they felt no pain they would sleep right through it. They would wake in the morning with part of their body gone unless someone was there to watch over them.

The first sign of leprosy was regarded as a death sentence. "The person who has the leprous disease shall wear torn clothes and let the hair of his head be disheveled; and he shall cover his upper lip and cry out, 'Unclean, unclean.' He shall remain unclean as long as he has the disease; he is unclean. He shall live alone; his dwelling shall be outside the camp."

The law was quite clear: "Don't touch." The rabbis carried this much further. If a leper came into someone's house, the home itself was said to be defiled; it should be destroyed. If a leper was seen on a public street it was considered permissible to pelt him with eggs or even stones. To touch a leper was to become defiled yourself.

Imagine the thought of never being touched again: never to feel the hug of a little child, the hand of a friend grasping yours, the embrace of your spouse, the arm of your father draped across your shoulder.

And leprosy was not just a physical disease, it carried a moral stigma too. It was assumed to be a curse from God. Other diseases were said to be healed; leprosy had to be cleansed. Lepers were not just sick; they were considered "unclean," defiled.

That's why the gospel of Mark tells us the leper came "begging and kneeling" before Jesus. That's why the leper says to

Jesus, "If you *choose*, you can make me clean." The father of a demon-possessed child says to Jesus, "If you are *able*. . . ." The leper has no doubts about whether Jesus *could* cleanse him. He just doubts that Jesus would *want* to. He has a deep sense of unworthiness. He is overcome with shame.

This is not just a nice story about a healing, it is a disease out of our headlines. Think of a disease in our day that's highly contagious, that creates great fear, that's understood to be fatal, that carries a moral stigma. How would Jesus respond to such a one?

I got a phone call once from a woman whose family attended a church I had served years earlier. She asked me to visit her brother in the hospital, and although I knew her family fairly well, I was surprised, because I had never heard she had a brother.

He was dying of AIDS, having been sick for quite some time. He had gone for a year without any conversation at all with his parents, and his primary goal had been to die unnoticed and alone. But finally his sister found out that he was ill and convinced him to go to the hospital.

He spoke of trying to kill himself at night because he was so filled with horror and shame. He made peace with God, however, and asked me to baptize him. So I did, with his sister watching, just a few days before he died.

His parents visited him a few times in the hospital, but they would not acknowledge the reason he was there. His mother, the woman who had brought his body into the world, refused to touch it now as he was about to leave. Her primary concern was to make sure that in any public records the cause of death would not be listed as AIDS, so that no one would know. She refused to speak the word.

He died without ever receiving from his mother or father the touch that might have helped to heal his soul.

The religious leaders of Jesus' day chose what might be called a strategy of isolation. Lepers, Gentiles, tax collectors, women, the uncircumcised — all these were to be avoided "like the plague." They would not eat with, talk with, work with, or look at them. There was one group of rabbis called the "bruised and bleeding" rabbis, who committed themselves to never even look at a woman. They figured this was the best way to beat lust. If they thought they saw a woman out of the corner of their eye they would close their eyes until they were sure she was out of sight. This caused them to be forever running into objects and buildings, hence the title "bruised and bleeding" rabbis. I'm not making this up.

The idea behind the strategy of isolation is that sin and suffering are contagious. The way to avoid them is to separate yourself from the kind of people and places where you might be exposed. Live in a spiritual quarantine.

I understand the appeal of this strategy. Sin spreads like the common cold. Get around a group of complainers, and what do you start to do? We live in a world that is surely as morally polluted as it is physically.

When I look at my kids, and think about how the world is so full of destructiveness, I'd love to be able to quarantine them.

> In isolation love dies; humility and compassion and generosity of spirit all suffocate.

Put a big sign around their necks: *If you're into substance abuse, casual sex, destruction of property, dropping out, or bizarre body piercing, keep away. Don't touch. Quarantine.* But it just doesn't work that way.

Throughout history religious people have been attracted to the strategy of isolation: avoid sinful people and live in religious quarantine. The problem is when I do this I come to view the world as "us" versus "them." The quarantine becomes a greenhouse for the most destructive sins: pride, exclusivism, self-righteousness. In isolation love dies; humility and compassion and generosity of spirit all suffocate. The ultimate outcome of the strategy of isolation is seen in places like the former

Yugoslavia where genocide is euphemized as "ethnic *cleansing*." People who are different, "other," are seen as filth that needs to be removed.

In Jesus, God makes it clear that he has forever rejected the strategy of isolation. There are several miracles in this story; the first begins here.

THE MIRACLE OF THE APPROACHABILITY

JESUS WAS A RABBI. A rabbi's job was to make sure the law was understood and followed.

This man was a leper. It was a leper's job to avoid all people, especially rabbis. A rabbi was the last person a leper wanted to see. If he got close to a rabbi he knew he'd get hammered for breaking the law: he had it coming.

Rabbis prided themselves on being unapproachable. They thought of themselves as being so close to God that common sinners — lepers, the unclean — should not be allowed to get too close.

The irony is that the only rabbi the leper could approach was God himself.

What quality did Jesus have that the other rabbis did not? He was eminently approachable. Not just with lepers. This happened on a regular basis with prostitutes and tax collectors and gentile pagans — with rag dolls of all kinds. The more religious the rabbis became, the more unapproachable they were.

We face the same problem. We know it is important to be holy, so we begin to try to impress people with our theological knowledge or moral purity to reinforce our own sense of spiritual superiority. If we keep it up, it isn't long before we, too, become unapproachable.

Here is one of the fundamental ways to distinguish between Jesus' way of life and that of the religious leaders. For them, the more spiritual they became the less approachable they were. But with Jesus, it was just the opposite. Jesus had the kind of profound "differentness" that drew sinners to him. The Pharisees had the kind of superficial differentness that pushed people away.

When I was growing up I often thought that the more "spiritual" a person was, the more unapproachable they were, that holiness involved a certain rigidity and sternness and distance.

But in Jesus we see that true spirituality always makes a person *more* approachable, not less. That's why it is worth reflecting on this: *Jesus is the most approachable human being that ever lived.*

It is in the act of touch that we become most present and real to each other. Some years ago we took our three children to Disneyland, and Mickey Mouse came out to greet the public. All the kids wanted the same thing. They didn't ask for gifts or free passes. They wanted to be touched. Our youngest child jumped up and down and began to shout over and over, "Touch me, touch me."

> Jesus had the kind of profound "differentness" that drew sinners to him.

Belle, the star of *Beauty and the Beast*, came out. Our two daughters jumped up and down and began to shout over and over, "Touch me, touch me."

(A little while later we saw Kevin Costner there with his children. My wife jumped up and down and began to shout. . . .)

Mark tells of one time when a group of little children were brought to see Jesus "in order that he might *touch* them." The disciples tried to keep them away and "spoke sternly" to them. They understood that someone as important as Jesus is generally not approachable. But Jesus was indignant. "And he took them up in his arms, laid his hands on them, and blessed them." He didn't have to. He could have just spoken a few words. But instead he gave them a gift. Imagine being one of those children, being able to remember the rest of your life that you had been touched by Jesus.

One of the most important diagnostic questions I can ask myself is "Am I becoming *more* or *less* approachable?" How *available* am I to the people in my little world? Can my spouse say *anything* to me? Do I sometimes pause to put a hand on the shoulder of the people I work with, just to let them know I'm glad they're there? Am I getting better at listening to people without judging them?

> One of the most important diagnostic questions I can ask myself is "Am I becoming *more* or *less* approachable?"

THE MIRACLE OF THE TOUCH

THE SECOND MIRACLE HAS to do with the order of events. The law said, "Don't touch." The Gospels are full of stories about people who sought to touch Jesus: little children, the woman suffering from hemorrhages who desperately grasped the hem of his garment, the prostitute who anointed Jesus' feet with her tears and wiped them with her hair, and doubting Thomas, who demanded to feel Jesus' wounds with his own hands.

Unlike all of these, the leper made no attempt to touch Jesus. The leper understood the situation. He knew the law.

But notice what Jesus did: "Moved with pity, Jesus stretched out his hand and touched him, and said to him, 'I do choose. Be made clean!'"

Jesus touched the leper *before* he healed him. He touched the leper *while the leper was still unclean*. This would have scandalized anyone who watched. To touch a leper was to be regarded as unclean yourself. This was a great miracle. This is God, who, after all, *made* the law, breaking his own law, for the sake of humanity. Jesus did not need to touch the leper to cleanse him. He performed other miracles at a distance; all he had to do was "say the word." The word healed his body, but the touch healed his soul. But Jesus wanted something understood.

The miracle of the touch is that Jesus was willing to share another person's suffering in order to bring about healing. This is a foreshadowing of the cross: Jesus taking on our sin so that we could take on his life. By his stripes we are healed.

In a contagious world, we learn to keep our distance. If we get too close to those who are suffering, we might get infected by their pain. It may not be convenient or comfortable. But only when you get close enough to catch their hurt will they be close enough to catch your love.

> The miracle of the touch is that Jesus was willing to share another person's suffering in order to bring about healing.

Jesus did not call his followers to live in quarantine. He called them to be a kind of hospital. Imagine a hospital where the doctors say, "This has been a successful day. I wasn't infected. My patients were loaded with filthy germs, but I kept them all outside. They may be dying, but at least *I* didn't touch any of them. I didn't get infected."

Years ago Nancy and I were about to enter an antique shop when she pulled me aside. I had our baby daughter in a contraption suspended from my back, and Nancy was eight months pregnant with another one. "Maybe you'd better stay outside," she said. "I've been inside this place before. I've seen the price tags. They have valuable pieces in there. There are signs all over the place: 'Don't touch.' And I know you. You'll go over to the rare books section and forget you have a baby on your back, and when you stop paying attention she'll break an incredibly expensive vase, and it will cost a fortune."

"Excuse me," I said. "I'm thirty years old, and I have a doctorate in psychology. I think I'll be able to handle a one-year-old for half an hour."

"Fine. But I want it mutually understood that if she breaks something, it will come out of your allowance for the next twenty years."

We went inside.

I found the rare book section and started reading.

I forgot all about the baby on my back.

She lunged for something. I gasped. Nancy heard it and whirled around. But being eight months pregnant, her body extended far beyond its normal boundaries. She ended up knocking an incredibly expensive vase to the ground, shattering it.

That was ten years ago. She's still paying.

Every day you and I walk through God's shop. Every day we brush up against objects of incalculable worth to him. People. Every one of them carries a price tag, if only we could see it. Lepers and AIDS patients, children and gray panthers, the wise and the foolish, saints and prostitutes: Worth the life of my Son, the price tag says. Will you respect the value of those you touch? Are you willing to pay the price? When you reach out to the untouchables in your world, you are signing up for pain. Love means disappointment and heartache.

But what is the alternative? C. S. Lewis wrote,

> To love at all is to be vulnerable. Love anything, and your heart will certainly be wrung and possibly be broken. If you want to make sure of keeping it intact, you must give your heart to no one, not even to an animal. Wrap it carefully round with hobbies and little luxuries; avoid all entanglements; lock it up safe in the casket or coffin of your selfishness. But in that casket — safe, dark, motionless, airless — it will change. It will not be broken; it will become unbreakable, impenetrable, irredeemable. The alternative to tragedy, or at least to the risk of tragedy, is damnation. The only place outside Heaven where you can be perfectly safe from all the dangers and perturbations of love is Hell.

For God's shop is full of signs that say please touch. We may not want to. We are afraid or shy or busy. But it is only when people are touched in their brokenness that healing comes.

Today there will be people in your world waiting for someone to touch them.

Today there will be people in your world waiting for someone to touch them. Will you be the one? Put an arm around the shoulder of a friend. Take the hand of someone who hurts. Embrace a child. Please touch.

THE IMMACULATE INFECTION

No one would touch a leper, because everybody knew what would happen. Touching a leper meant being infected with leprosy. So it had always been — at least people thought.

But something stronger than leprosy is at work in this story. Mark says Jesus touched the man and "immediately" the leprosy left him. The leper did not infect Jesus with his sickness. Jesus infected the leper with his life! This is what might be called the immaculate infection. The life that flooded in and through Jesus was so strong that leprosy simply could not coexist with it.

Sin and suffering are not all that is contagious. Thank God. So is enthusiasm and laughter and faith itself. Get around someone who has them and you discover they're catching. Contagion works both ways.

Jesus twice used the image of yeast in his teaching. Yeast is a picture of contagion. Put a little lump in a batch of dough and soon the whole thing is leavened. In Matthew 16 he warned his followers to beware the yeast of the Pharisees. Their judgmental spirit about who is touchable and who is not will spread. Sin is that way. We know that, and we reflect it in a dozen proverbs: *One bad apple spoils the whole bunch. Bad company corrupts morals.* The Pharisees had been inoculated with just enough religion to avoid catching a full-blown case of what Jesus was spreading. They had enough of a dose of self-righteousness to be inoculated against faith.

But in Matthew 13 Jesus used yeast to describe something else: the kingdom of God. This time he gave measurements: he spoke of a woman mixing yeast into an amount of flour so vast as to be absurd, as if she were working with industrial sacks of flour, making a meal for Cleveland. The yeast looks overmatched. In fact the literal language of the text is that she "hid" the leaven in the flour. It seems to be an exercise in futility. The yeast apparently just disappears. But only be patient. Unseen, unobserved, that yeast is permeating the whole batch. The flour doesn't stand a chance. It's just a matter of time, now.

So it is with the kingdom of God, Jesus says. It cannot be stopped. Ever since Jesus, the yeast has been at work. It may look small and insignificant: a storefront church in a burned-out inner-city neighborhood, a house church meeting underground in China, a small group praying for their little corner of the world. It may look unimpressive now, like a lump of yeast Jesus says, but you keep watching. Only be patient. The darkness doesn't stand a chance. It's just a matter of time.

> The secret is to be so filled with the life of Jesus that in touching the world, instead of its infecting us, we infect it.

The secret to spiritual life is not to isolate yourself from sin and suffering. That would be impossible, even if we wanted to. Jesus lived on the same contaminated planet as the rest of us, but he was immune. Our systems, however, have broken down.

The secret is to be so filled with the life of Jesus that in touching the world, instead of its infecting us, we infect it.

The ex-leper had the bug. He was contagious; he just couldn't help it. Even though he's warned to be silent, he finds he can't. His faith was so infectious that Mark says the word "spread," like a germ, like a bad cold, like a hot rumor. Everybody caught it. "People came to him from every corner."

And ever since then those who have been touched by Jesus have gone out spreading germs. Little joy germs, faith germs, belief bacteria.

For we live, as my friend Ian Pitt-Watson said in a wonderful treatment of this passage, on a contaminated planet. It is contaminated on every level. It should have been quarantined from heaven. No reasonable God would go near it with a ten-foot pole.

But Jesus is not a reasonable God. He became a human being, he took on your uncleanness and mine. But instead of the world infecting him, he infected the world. With his immaculate infection. It's still spreading.

It's just a matter of time.

Four

The Lord of the
Second Chance

Forgiveness is God's invention for coming to terms with a world in which people are unfair to each other and hurt each other deeply. He began by forgiving us. And he invites us all to forgive each other.

Lewis B. Smedes

A few years ago I went to play golf with some friends (something I do very rarely and very badly). On the first hole, I lined up to hit the ball, which looks so easy when it's done on TV. After all, the ball is not even moving. I hit a shank which defied belief. It went off at a ninety-degree angle. It was astounding. No one had ever seen a golf ball go off at that trajectory before, and we weren't sure up to that point that it was physically possible. I wished so badly I could have that one back again. (It hit the slate roof of a nearby townhome and sounded like it may have done some damage.)

I started to try to track the ball down so I could hit my next shot, when the people I was playing with said an amazing thing: "Don't bother. Let it go." They told me to take what is called a *mulligan*. You don't have to play the unplayable lie, they said. You don't even have to count it. We won't write it down. It won't appear on the score card. It will be as if it never happened, they said. Irrelevant to my ultimate score. I was given a clean slate. A fresh beginning.

I could start over — as if for the first time. A mulligan is a kind of grace note in an otherwise unforgiving game.

And I started thinking, *Wouldn't it be wonderful to be able to take mulligans in other areas of life?* Imagine: a policeman stops you for speeding, you just tear the ticket up. Thanks officer, I'll be taking my mulligan. Right you are, he says.

The bank tells you your check bounced. Mulligan, you tell them. No problem, they say.

In an argument with a friend, you say something you shouldn't. Mulligan.

Botch a test, blow a presentation at work, invest in the wrong company, commit an embarrassing faux pas, forget to send in taxes: Just take a mulligan.

No questions asked.

No penalties assigned.

The truth is, rag dolls need mulligans all the time. I have a chance to serve someone and I do something self-promoting instead. I allow a deceptive statement to stand in order to get credit that doesn't belong to me. I blow up for no good reason. Tucking in one of my children after an episode of this I made confession: "I'm sorry I was so crabby. I don't know what got into me. I hope Santa still brings me a present."

A sad but doubtful shaking of the child's head. "I hope he does too."

Does Santa give mulligans?

Sometimes the need for a mulligan runs deeper. Sometimes you need a mulligan for whole eras of your life. A woman had a complicated, conflict-filled relationship with her dad — she loved him but was angry at him, and her response was to withdraw. Finally, in another part of the country, her dad died alone, and now she's filled with such regret. She'd give anything for a mulligan.

You take a course of action — make a choice — that wounds somebody close to you, somebody who really matters to you. And now you are eaten up by guilt; you don't know if the trust level can ever be restored — you'd give anything for a mulligan.

You're involved in a dishonest financial practice. Now you live in fear of being found out, disgraced; you live in awareness that your life has been built on deception and fraud. Maybe nobody will ever know, but your own conscience and moral sensitivity are being eroded day by day. Your dishonesty is like a spiritual cancer destroying your soul. You need a mulligan more than you know.

> If there is one way that human beings consistently underestimate God's love, it is perhaps in his loving longing to forgive.

You fail at something that matters — at your life's work or your marriage or parenting or expressing integrity — and the sense of failure won't go away. You feel tainted by it, feel like you will never be free. It clings to you like your very skin, and you despair of ever starting over. If only you could take a mulligan.

If there is one way that human beings consistently underestimate God's love, it is perhaps in his loving longing to forgive. In his wonderful novel *Cold Mountain* Charles Frazier writes of a minister named Monroe who is shunned by his peers because of his "failure to believe in a God with severe limitations on His patience and mercy. Monroe had in fact preached that God was not at all such a one as ourselves, not one to be temperamentally inclined to tread ragefully upon us until our blood flew up and stained all His white raiment. . . ."

BROKEN BY FAILURE

JOHN'S GOSPEL TELLS THE STORY of a man who failed his best friend, who denied his master; who thought his failure put him beyond the reach of God's grace, and who turned out to be blessedly, wonderfully wrong. It is a story for anyone who has ever been broken by failure.

It is the story of the raggedness of man and the greatness of God.

This is a story about a man who threw away the chance of a lifetime. And this is a story about the Lord of the second chance.

It is 6:00 A.M. Peter and his friends have been fishing all night. They've caught nothing.

A figure calls to them from shore. A Voice they have heard before but don't recognize yet says, "Children, you haven't caught anything, have you?"

The question has a little sting to it. It is designed to see if they'll acknowledge reality — failure.

Jesus often uses casual statements or questions to see if people will acknowledge truth about themselves: "What were you talking about on the way?" he said to the disciples when they were arguing about who was the greatest. "Where is your husband?" he asked the woman married five times. "How's it going?" he questions here. "Catch anything?"

He softens the sting a little by the way he addresses his friends: "Children." It is the only time he addresses them this way in the Gospels. "Well, boys, any luck?"

And a remarkable thing happens: A group of fishermen admit they haven't caught anything. They don't even comment on the one that got away. (Fishermen do not generally have a reputation for being the most truthful of sportsmen.)

The Voice says, *Catch anything?*

No, they say. *What's your point, Voice?* The story starts with an admission of failure, and that's all he's waiting to hear.

The Voice says, *Try again. Put your net down on the right side of the boat. Don't quit yet. Give it another try.*

They do. And soon the net is so full they can't lift it back up into the boat. Suddenly they realize whom the voice belongs to.

Peter is filled with emotion. He may be recalling the time when he first met Jesus.

Luke tells the story: Jesus got in Peter's boat and taught the crowd on shore, then he said to Peter, "Put your boat in deep water and let down your nets."

Peter explains, "We fished all night, didn't catch a thing. . . ."

Try again. Humor me.

So Peter did, and soon the nets were so full that they began to break, the boats so full of fish they began to sink.

That very first time Peter said to Jesus, "Go away from me, Lord, for I am a sinful man!" Ragged people pray that sometimes.

> If you're going to receive help from the Lord of the second chance, you too will have to acknowledge the truth about your condition.

But Jesus said, I know all about your being a sinful man. I've got plans to help you with that problem. I'm giving you a new life. You're going to begin again, but this time you're going to fish for people.

So Peter met the Lord of the second chance.

Now, after the crucifixion and the resurrection, after another fishing miracle, Peter realizes whom the voice belongs to. In typical Petrine fashion he kicks off his blue jeans and the lucky fishing shirt he never washes and jumps into the water and swims ashore. Maybe he remembers another time he left his friends in the boat and walked on the water. His faith gave out and he sank — he failed — but the Lord of the second chance rescued him then, too. He's very patient, the Lord of the second chance.

Peter got to the shore and found Jesus fixing breakfast. He had started a fire. John includes a detail: it was a charcoal fire.

There was a reason for this. In John 18, when Peter was asked three times if he knew Jesus, if he was a disciple, he was warming himself in front of a fire. We're told it was a charcoal fire. And that was where he denied his Lord.

Now Peter sees the fire, a charcoal fire, and he remembers. If he's going to be with Jesus, he'll have to face the truth about who he is and what he's done.

If you're going to receive help from the Lord of the second chance, you too will have to acknowledge the truth about your condition. Face up to reality. Take off the mask.

There is an old story about a man desperate for a job, who responds to a want ad at the zoo. The warden explains that their gorilla has died; they can't afford a new one, so they'll pay this man to dress up like one. He balks at first, but needing the money badly he finally agrees.

Each day he gets a little more enthusiastic in his cage. One day he swings on a vine so hard he ends up in the cage next door: the lion's cage. Feeling the lion's hot breath on his face he forgets his disguise and begins to scream for help. At which point the lion says, "Shut up, you idiot, or we'll both lose our jobs."

Wearing masks can become a way of life. Pretending to be happy when you carry a secret ache. Pretending to be spiritually healthy when there is a great distance between you and God. Pretending to have a perfect marriage when the truth is your relationship has a hollow chamber where its heart should be.

Peter remembers now the great failure of his life. He had lots of failures: the time when he sank in the water, the time when Jesus said he was speaking the words of Satan, the time when he tried to rescue Jesus with a sword and performed history's first recorded ear amputation, but this was the great failure. Sometimes in life you have one like this. It feels irredeemable. Unforgivable.

He remembers when he stood by the fire and failed his God.

Breakfast is over now, and they're standing by the fire, just Peter and Jesus.

Alone together perhaps for the first time since the denial, crucifixion, and resurrection. Peter is so vulnerable; he waits for Jesus' words like a prisoner waiting to hear the verdict of court.

Then he hears the question that would wound him to the heart; the question that would heal him and bring him back to life, the question he would carry to his grave.

Do you love me?

Jesus doesn't ask, "Peter, are you sorry for what you've done? Do you promise never to fail me again? Will you try harder?"

New Testament scholar Murray Harris puts it this way in regard to this story: "First things first."

Do you love me?

This is such a tender question. When you ask this question, your heart is on the line. This is the question of a hopeful lover. It is the question a parent longs to ask a runaway child, but is afraid to ask too.

Do you love me?

Tevye, the milkman whose daughters defy the matchmaker to marry for love, sits with his wife one day, strangely shy, and asks her in song because the question is too tender to be merely spoken: "Golde, do you love me?"

"Do I *what?*" she asks.

"Do you love me?"

She is not prepared for this discussion. She did the things a wife was supposed to do in that culture. Fulfilled obligations. Maintained the household. End of discussion.

Again the question: "Do you love me?"

She tells him he's a fool. He agrees, but still he wants an answer.

"Do I love him?" she muses, partly to him, partly to herself. She reviews twenty-five years of life — hope and suffering and fighting and sharing home and bed. If that's not love — what is?

"Then . . ." (like a little kid he says it. Like a young lover) . . . you love me!"

"I suppose I do."

"And I suppose I love you too."

"It doesn't change a thing," they sing together, "but even so, after twenty-five years, it's nice to know."

It doesn't change a thing — they still have the same tasks to do, a life to lead — but it changes everything.

The two of them sit on the little bench and hold hands. The relationship they thought was just arranged, just completing tasks and fulfilling obligations, has become a love story. Their hearts are so full they can't speak.

Do you love me?

This is Jesus' question, and it is not an easy or comfortable question for me to answer honestly. Sometimes I think about Jesus, how good and wise he was — and I know he is wonderful, that his offer, his word is the best chance humanity will ever have.

I know I do.

But sometimes, the truth is, I'm so full of myself I don't know if I *really* love.

Now it's just Jesus and Peter before a little fire, a charcoal fire. "Simon, son of John . . ." Jesus doesn't even use his old nickname, Peter. He uses his formal name, as if to say, "I won't presume that you want the old intimate relationship. I won't presume you still want to wear the name I gave you.

"Simon, son of John, do you love me?"

Now Jesus is the vulnerable one. Now Jesus is the Lover waiting to hear the response of the one he loves.

"Yes Lord," Peter answers, but he doesn't fully trust his ability to assess even his own heart. You know everything. You know.

I understand Peter's answer: Lord, you know. As best I can, I do love you. When I'm in my right mind, I do. I want to, better than I do now. I don't even know the whole truth about my heart. Lord, you know.

"Then feed my sheep," Jesus says. Love and teach and guard and guide and serve the little flock that means all the world to me. Get back in the game.

Three time this is repeated, until Peter is hurt. Why does Jesus keep asking? People sometimes find significance in the fact that John uses a different Greek word for love in Jesus' third question, as if Jesus were going to settle for an inferior kind of love from

Peter. But the general consensus of New Testament scholars is that John is simply using "stylistic variation," to keep from repeating the same word over and over.

The significance of the repetition is not in the synonyms but in the number of times the question is repeated. Three times. Peter does not know what we do, that he is being healed by the Lord of the second chance.

Not once but three times he stood by the fire and denied his Lord; not once but three times he stands by the fire and professes his love.

Jesus says to Peter, Jesus says to everyone who's ever stood by the fire and failed God, Jesus says still to you and me whatever we've done, Get back in the game. Nurture the gifts I gave you and cherish the calling I gave you and devote yourself to the church. Feed my sheep. They need you.

In the movie *City Slickers* Billy Crystal is trying to console his friend, a character whose life is in shambles — his marriage is over, his career is destroyed — and who is ready to end it all.

Billy Crystal tells him, "Take a do-over. Like when we were kids playing a game and things went badly — we'd just start over again. You can do it now. Take a do-over."

But where do we get the power and the right for do-overs?

I shanked another ball and my friends said the same thing: "Take another mulligan."

"Are you sure?"

"Of course," they said. "We do it all the time."

At this point, I got a little concerned for the integrity of the game. If you just keep on taking mulligans, the score doesn't really mean anything. Especially if, like me, you hit a lot of bad shots. I hit balls into the water, out of bounds; I used up four mulligans on the first hole.

The reason we were so liberal with mulligans that day was because the game didn't count. We weren't really taking it seriously.

We just wanted to have a good score. When it comes to keeping score, golfers usually hold to a level of truth telling, honesty, and integrity held by loan sharks and bookies. Golfers make fishermen look honest. The truth is, we can agree not to write down a shot, but we're not really fooling anybody.

However, when the game counts, it's a different story. When the game counts, there must be justice. If you're playing Tiger Woods for the Masters and you're tied on the final hole and you shank your drive, you can't say, "I believe I'll take a mulligan here."

> The place where God's unswerving commitment to justice and God's undying longing to forgive meet is the cross.

There are no mulligans on the PGA tour. The integrity of the game counts. The rules matter. This is the real thing. You play the ball where it lies. Hit it in the water you take the penalty. Reap what you sow. There must be justice. Your score is a brutally honest reflection of what you did.

You understand the point. Life matters. The rules count — the important ones do. If God is any kind of God, he must be just. He can't say, "Hitler, take a mulligan. We just won't count the Holocaust. Won't write it down. Let's pretend it never happened."

Someone must keep score — of the Dachaus and the Tienanmen Squares and the Bosnias and the drive-by shootings and abused children and the oppressed poor of this world. There must one day be justice for this world to make any sense at all. And the Bible says there will be. The Bible says justice will roll like a river one day. We will all give an account for the sin and wrongdoing in our lives — and that includes you and me. We will all sign the scorecard.

The Bible says the place where God's unswerving commitment to justice and God's undying longing to forgive meet is the cross. The cross is the declaration of God's hatred of sin and all the damage sin does. The cross is the declaration of God's love for sinners and his insatiable appetite to redeem them.

The Bible is full of pictures of God's longing to give second chances. "As a father has compassion for his children, so the LORD has compassion for those who fear him."

We used to have a bedtime ritual when my children were small. "I don't love you this much," I'd say, holding my hands a few inches apart, "and I don't love you this much [hands a foot apart now], or this much, or this much" (the gap growing wider until it was as far as my arms could go). "I love you *this much*."

Occasionally, they would test it. We were washing the car when one of my children got into the trunk, put all its contents on the ground, and sprayed them thoroughly: books, blankets, my tennis racquet, and a new dress were all hosed and sudsed up beyond recognition. My daughter, who was about four at the time, could see from my face that she had sinned, and the wages of sin is death. She looked up with big brown eyes and threw her arms out to the side as far as she could: "I love you this much."

How could I punish that? "All right, honey. Let's just put this stuff in the garage."

I could forgive her, but of course someone's got to pay for the damage. She has incurred debt for books and clothes and racquet, and if I cleaned out her whole piggy bank it wouldn't make a dent in what she owes. Forgiving is never just a matter of words, there is a cost attached. Someone has to pay the debt.

> The first question is not how much do you love God? The first question is how much does God love you?

This is what happened at the cross, the Bible says. In some way we will never fully understand, an unpayable debt was paid. And we can start over. We must.

The first question is not how much do you love God? The first question is how much does God love you?

God filled the world with beauty and mystery, with waterfalls and sunsets and glaciers and tropics and banana cream pie, but God said, "I don't just love you this much."

God gave you a mind, the ability to know right from wrong, to choose good, life, but God said, "I don't just love you this much."

God gave you people. Teachers, friends, heroes, persons with whom to know the joy of intimacy and community. But God said, "I don't just love you this much."

Then God gave Jesus. Jesus was God's ultimate attempt to let us know what we mean to him. He was led to the cross to pay the debt we couldn't. He was led to the cross and God said, "Now you can be freed from every regret. No more guilt. Every demand of justice satisfied. Now at last you understand the place you have in my heart."

He was led to the cross and Jesus said, "I love you this much."

And now it was Peter's turn to learn the Lord of the cross is the Lord of the second chance.

Warren Bennis wrote about a promising junior executive at IBM who was involved in a risky venture for the company and ended up losing ten million dollars in the gamble. He was called into the office of Tom Watson Sr., the founder and leader of IBM for forty years, a business legend.

The junior exec, overwhelmed with guilt and fear, blurted out: "I guess you've called me in for my resignation. Here it is. I resign."

Watson replied, "You must be joking. I just invested ten million dollars educating you; I can't afford your resignation."

I imagine Peter must have had this conversation with Jesus on a regular basis.

Peter made his famous confession that Jesus was the Christ, the Son of the living God. Jesus called him blessed, said that this had been revealed to Peter by God himself, and went on to explain that it was necessary for him to go to the cross. When Peter took him aside and "began to rebuke" him for this ("it's bad for morale"), Jesus told him that Peter was now speaking the words of Satan.

I imagine Peter saying, "You're right about me. I speak impulsively; I'm always putting my foot in my mouth. Here's my resignation."

And I imagine Jesus saying, "You must be joking. I've just invested a revelation in you. I can't afford your resignation."

On the Sea of Galilee Peter hops out of the boat, begins to walk on the water. But he takes his eyes off Jesus. He is overwhelmed by fear and doubt and would have drowned had not Jesus bailed him out. Jesus diagnoses his problem acutely: "You of little faith."

I imagine Peter saying, "You're right about me. I'm big on dramatic gestures, but I don't trust very well. Inside I'm full of questions and fears. It doesn't take much of a storm to stop me. Here's my resignation."

"You must be joking. I've just invested a miracle in you. I can't afford your resignation."

Peter said, at the great crisis of Jesus' life, "I'll follow you, no matter how much it costs, no matter what everybody else does."

But he could not even follow for one night. He denied his best friend three times.

> The church is a place for people who need do-overs. That is what God does.

I imagine him saying, "You were right about me all along. I failed you most completely at your point of greatest need. I denied and abandoned you. Here's my resignation."

And Jesus said, "You must be joking. I've just invested a resurrection in you. I can't afford your resignation."

The church is a place for people who need do-overs. That is what God does.

He comes to old father Abraham who laughs at God's promise and lies about his wife and God says: "How about a do-over?"

To a shepherd boy who became king and committed murder and adultery; to a prophet who ran away and was rescued from the belly of a fish and wanted to die because he had to sit in the hot sun with no vine; to a whole nation of stiff-necked and idolatrous people; to a persecutor named Saul who mocked his Son and terrorized his people; to desperate, lonely, sinful people God comes again and again and again and says, "How about a do-over?"

For redeeming is what God is into. He is the finder of directionally-challenged sheep, the searcher of missing coins, the embracer of foolish prodigal sons. His favorite department is Lost and Found.

> His love has no limits,
> his grace has no measure,
> his power has no boundaries known unto men.

He redeems and redeems and redeems and is present right now as you read these words, and he longs to do for you what he has done for countless rag dolls before you.

He is the God of the do-over; the Lord of the second chance.

Take a mulligan.

F I V E

JESUS THE TEACHER

*While Jesus was not a philosopher or theologian, his parables
alone provide material that neither the philosopher nor the
theologian can exhaust. This is the mark of Jesus' supreme genius. We have a curious tendency, even in dealing with Jesus'
humanity, to overlook his sheer intellectual stature.*

C. W. F. SMITH

I met Mrs. Beier thirty years ago. For five years she taught piano
lessons to my sister and me.

Mrs. Beier was German, thoroughly and hopelessly German.
And when I've told you she's German, I've told you everything
about her you need to know.

For five years, she dominated the life of my family. Other
piano teachers in Rockford set the bar pretty low: Practice when
you can, progress at your own pace. With Mrs. Beier it was not
that way, none of this Rogerian, non-directive, child-centered
molly-coddling. If you were her student, you did what she said.

We practiced what she told us to practice, for as long as she
told us to practice. If she told us to do scales a half-hour a day,
we did scales a half-hour a day. We set the metronome at her
tempo. We sat in the approved posture, we curved our fingers
at the precise angle she specified. We cut our fingernails short to
avoid clicking them on the keys, which was not the favored length
for my sister when she hit adolescence.

There was something about Mrs. Beier that made you take her seriously as a teacher. She told my parents one time that our current piano at home was inadequate, that they needed to buy a new piano.

They bought a new piano.

We finally reached a point during our teenage years when we were doing too many other things, and we didn't want to be her students any longer. It was time to quit. The problem was, nobody dared to tell Mrs. Beier! We weren't sure she'd let us quit. We sat around the dinner table one night, and my parents said to each other, "This is ridiculous." Finally, my dad offered me five dollars to call her up and tell her the bad news over the phone. Since those unfortunately were the days before answering machines, I had to do it live.

Lest I give the wrong impression, let me hasten to add that learning from Mrs. Beier was not simply an act of drudgery. Sometimes it involved practicing when I didn't feel like it, but often it produced great joy. One overriding reality kept me in the game: She could make music like no one I had ever known.

Until I met her, I didn't think it was possible that a real flesh-and-blood human being could do that. Sometimes we'd come in and she'd just have us sit down, and she'd play Mozart, Beethoven, or (her favorite) Rachmaninoff, and it was as if we'd been transported to another world.

Then she would tell us what we hardly dared believe. "If you'll trust me," she'd say, "if you will put yourself in my hands, if you'll do what I tell you to do, one day you'll be able to do what I do. One day the music will be in you."

I was too young or too unobservant to notice it at the time, but when she was not playing the piano Mrs. Beier's fingers were normally cramped and twisted, as if she were getting ready to claw something. She was severely arthritic. She could not hit a single note without pain. To play entire scores of Rachmaninoff, as she did for us until the Steinway shook, must have been agony. But she did it because she loved the music. And she did it for us. She wanted us to be captivated by the beauty of it all, as she was; she wanted to give us this great gift, so she endured pain we could not even imagine.

Like every great teacher, what moved her to teach was love. Her love for music. Her love for her students. Truly great teaching is always a form of love.

> Great teaching is always a form of love.

Every parent knows this. This is why parents buy educational toys, why they spend countless hours coaxing their children to sit up and stand up and take a step, why they cheer sounds coming from their infants that bear no resemblance to any recognizable word, why they put charts and artwork on the refrigerator, why they read to children and drag them off to lessons and let them "help" do things around the house that parents could do infinitely quicker on their own.

Great teaching is always a form of love. We see this in the story of Anne Sullivan who awakened the soul of Helen Keller. We see it in the ring of students surrounding Socrates as he was about to die, trying to express their love for him. It is what stirs us in movies such as *Mr. Holland's Opus* and *Dead Poets Society*. Great teachers do more than pass on information and catalogue facts. They see beyond our raggedness. They open us up — mind and heart — to a new world.

Jesus asks all who would be his followers to receive him as their teacher. He lived in a way that no flesh-and-blood human being had ever done. People who watched him and listened to him were transported to another world.

And then he said words they hardly dared to believe: Here's your chance, he said. If you'll trust me, if you'll do what I tell you to do, if you'll put your life in my hands, then one day you can live as I do. One day the music can be in you.

But first you must accept Jesus as your Teacher.

About a century ago, a debate about Jesus that had been going on for some time became much more prominent. One side in this debate said that the Jesus of history was simply a teacher, although a very important one and possibly a great one. Another group of voices said, "No, he was not simply a wise person. He really is divine. The Jesus of history really is the Son of God."

My own tradition and understanding says that the Jesus of the New Testament was both fully human and fully divine and is today living and vitally involved in human affairs.

But in this debate a bad thing happened. People who believe in the divinity of Jesus began to de-emphasize the role of Jesus' teaching ministry. There was an assumption that when people started talking about Jesus' teaching it was a kind of code for disbelieving in his divinity. Some branches of the church even claimed that large portions of his teaching, such as the Sermon on the Mount, did not even apply to the church today. So the importance of his teaching has been largely passed over.

But teaching is not just something Jesus did to pass the time until the crucifixion. It was not an optional, dispensable part of his ministry. When he taught he was not simply treading water until it was time to die.

His teaching was an irreplaceable part of his ministry. He came to teach us the way things are. Frederick Buechner writes:

> What is the kingdom of God? [Jesus] does not speak of a reorganization of society as a political possibility or of the doctrine of salvation as a doctrine. He speaks of what it is like to find a diamond ring that you thought you'd lost forever. He speaks of what it is like to win the Irish sweepstakes. He suggests rather than spells out. He evokes rather than explains. He catches by surprise. . . . It seems to me that more often than not the parables can be read as high and holy jokes

about God and about man and about the gospel itself as the highest and holiest joke of them all.

Jesus' followers were drawn to him largely because his teaching made so much sense. He was, among other things, simply the smartest man they had ever known. What he taught rang true with his own life and with the nature of how things are. They had never seen anyone live like him — had no idea that such a life was even a possibility. And he told him that if they trusted him, if they would put their lives in his hands, one day they would be able to have his kind of life as well. One day the music would be in them.

They discovered they could trust him as their teacher. And it was largely because they could trust him as their teacher that after his death and resurrection they were in a position to trust him as their Savior.

So if I want to fully experience the love of Jesus, I must receive one of the most important gifts he sends me — his teaching. I must invite Jesus to be the personal Teacher of my life. I must trust that he is right — about everything. And that therefore where I disagree with him I must either be wrong or not yet understand what it was he was saying. I must allow Jesus to teach me how to live.

Jesus himself told a story about the foundational importance of his teaching. It is one of his most famous stories. It is about the construction trade. This was a business with which he was intimately familiar, having taken over his dad's job as an independent contractor. It involves two men who build houses, but one builds on sand and the other on rock.

There is something universal about this story that causes it to keep popping up in various forms. A humble version of it is one of the best-known stories in American literature. It has inspired movies and songs and countless books. Here are the basic elements of the story. See if you can guess what it is:

- In this story the primary characters are builders — they each construct a house.

- Not all houses are created equal; there is a contrast between wise building and foolish building.
- Each house faces a test. If the house was built wisely, it stands; if it was built foolishly, it falls.

Sound familiar? It's the story of the three little pigs.

Each little pig built a house. One built with hay and straw, one built with sticks, one built with bricks, but they all built.

Each faced the big bad wolf. Each one heard the same polite plea for entrance, made the same defiant response ("not by the hair of my chinny chin chin . . ."), and faced the same threat from their pneumatically-enhanced enemy.

Two of the pigs built their house of junk. They never stopped to ask the question: "Will it stand up to wolf?" Only the house that was built with wisdom endures.

This is one of those parables in which Jesus really tells *two* stories — the story of a wise man and a foolish one. (Other examples would be the story about the father who asked his two sons to work in the field, or the story of the five wise and five foolish maidens.) Earl Palmer notes that the way to understand this type of parable is to set the two stories side by side and look at how they are alike and how they differ. When you see where they diverge, you see the point Jesus intended to make.

EACH PERSON BUILDS A HOUSE

This detail does not vary; this one is not optional: We are all house-builders.

To understand this, we could replace the word "house" with "character" or "soul." We are all of us constructing a life. We do this primarily, Palmer notes, by the choices we make.

Every commitment I make, every friendship I enter, every skill that I cultivate or neglect, every promise I honor or break, becomes a part of my house.

You are constructing your life. The quality of the choices you make will determine the quality of your character, your soul. The house is a common metaphor in the Bible.

There are various kinds of material that can be used to build on that foundation. Some use gold and silver and jewels; and some build with sticks, and hay, or even straw! There is going to come a time of testing at Christ's Judgment Day to see what kind of material each builder has used. Everyone's work will be put through the fire so that all can see whether or not it keeps its value, and what was really accomplished. Then every workman who has built on the foundation with the right materials, and whose work still stands, will get his pay. But if the house he has built burns up, he will have a great loss.

> The quality of the choices you make will determine the quality of your character, your soul.

We are each one of us responsible for our own house. No one else's.

But we have a hard time with this. We try to find someone else to make responsible for it. The wire services carried the story a few years ago of a man in Italy who was arrested for bigamy. In fact, he had 105 wives. When the authorities asked him how this had happened his response was that he had received bad legal advice. (It's hard to imagine what his lawyers might have said: "Try to keep a *reasonable* number of wives — a hundred or so. Just don't overdo it.")

This truth is so large that we may spend our whole lives evading it. Erich Fromm wrote in *Escape from Freedom* that many people refuse to truly make and own deep choices because they want to avoid the responsibility and anxiety that inevitably accompany human freedom. We see this in its extreme form in cults and communes. Authoritarian churches often flourish because many of us want someone to relieve us of the pressure of having to *choose*. But often our attempts to evade responsibility are more subtle.

A young woman chooses where she will go to school, what career she will enter, who she might date and marry all based on what she thinks her parents would want her to do. She never truly questions the beliefs, values, or religious convictions that her life is arranged around. Ironically, she doesn't even guess that her parents are much less certain of these things than she has always pictured them. Even her home is decorated in a way she thinks would be pleasing to them.

None of this is intentional. If asked, she would be adamant that she is "her own person." But the truth is she has abdicated her personhood. She is not building her own house. She is building someone else's. But she will have to live in it all the same.

Paul Tournier wrote, "To live is to choose. It is through the making of successive and resolute choices that man traces out his life."

Some people are so afraid of being disappointed by their choice they avoid making choices at all. But then that's the house you live in. Or you may fear disappointment so you procrastinate. Then you live in that house.

Here are some signs that I am failing to take responsibility for my own house:

- I am overly eager to please. I find myself looking for others' approval to validate my choices.
- I can't decide. I lack clarity on what it is that *I* truly think is right or good or even enjoyable. I waver and hesitate to commit.
- I am anxious. A little criticism from the wrong source leaves me feeling defeated.
- I lack integrity. Instead of freely saying what I believe, I calculate and adjust my words to fit more closely with what I think the other person wants to hear.

We are all house-builders. There is no alternative. We are constructing our lives.

EACH PERSON FACES THE STORM

There is another common feature: each person faces a storm. The wolf comes to the door of every little pig.

In fact, Jesus is quite explicit about this part of the story. His description of the storms that came to the two men is identical, word for word: "The rain came down, the streams rose, and the winds blew and beat against that house."

Jesus wants to make it clear: this is not a story about storm-avoidance. You cannot build a house where there will be no storms.

We would prefer a tale of two climates — two places with different weather, say, the Midwest and the Sunbelt. "And the house in Illinois was buried under snow, flooded by rain, battered by tornado; but the house in California mellowed in the surf and sun."

We'd like to find a neighborhood where the wolf would never knock at the door.

Our friends Richard and Elizabeth were as likely to find it as any. He's an attorney and she's a psychologist; they were attractive and prosperous and devoted to God and each other. They were married after being well established in their professional lives. Eventually the addition of a baby boy completed their happy if somewhat busy lives.

Richard suffered a fall riding a horse one day. The doctors at the emergency room X-rayed him, gave him something for the pain, told him to lay low for a few days, and sent him home. By the end of the weekend the pain was so intolerable he went back. This time a specialist took one look at the X-rays and blanched. He told Richard not to move, nod, or breathe any more than he needed to. It turned out he had suffered the same vertebrae injury that Christopher Reeve had, and that one wrong move or even sneeze could have resulted in permanent paralysis. What seemed like a charmed life was suddenly interrupted. They faced the possibility of life in a wheelchair for him, as well as the real possibility that he might die in surgery. But he didn't. A reprieve. All would be well. He went home and they were relieved and grateful people.

So relieved that they didn't think to have the results of another surgery checked. Just before the riding accident Richard had undergone a minor procedure (so the doctors always call it) to make sure they would have no more children. But in all the excitement of subsequent events they forgot to see if the procedure had had its desired effect.

It had not. They found out they were going to have another baby. This news was not altogether welcome, coming as it did into the lives of two busy forty-something types. But they were adjusting.

Then they got more news. The baby was not developing normally. Something was wrong. The child would be a victim of Down's syndrome.

This time there would be no reprieve. No corrective surgery would make everything the same as it was before.

Some well-meaning friends added to the pain: "God must have a special love for you, to give you such a gift." "Everyone is watching you, to see how you respond. I'm sure you'll do the right thing."

This is not a gift, it is a storm. There may be gifts that come in its wake, but it is a storm all the same. If you were to ask Elizabeth and Richard, they would tell you that this little life is unspeakably precious to them, that it has brought blessing and growth to their lives. But they would also tell you they'd trade that growth in a heartbeat if this little life could be given the healing and restoration and wholeness God intended all his children to have.

When I grew up I had the general idea that anything wrong that might happen to me would be fixable. If I lost something it could be found or replaced; if I failed at something my parents could set things right. But I have been in a few storms since then. I have learned that I was badly mistaken about this illusion of getting through life untouched. I look now at my family, my children, and wonder what will happen in the lives in my little house before they're through. And I'm glad I don't know. It's enough to know that there will be storms.

Jesus put it like this: "Don't worry about tomorrow. Tomorrow will worry about itself. Each day has troubles enough of its own." Trouble today, trouble tomorrow. That's the prediction.

STORMS TEST THE HOUSE

It is in the storm that the soundness of the house is revealed. A foundation is not a glamorous thing. No one visits a house and says, "What a great foundation you have here." No one even knows. Until the storm.

And the ultimate storm that Jesus referred to is the last judgment. One day our lives will be scrutinized by God. Every beam and timber, every word and deed will face scrupulous examination. One day the truth of our houses will be revealed.

Every decision I make goes into the building of my house, my life, so I cannot violate Jesus' teachings about the way things are and still have things come out all right. To do so is to try to saw against the grain of the universe.

Perhaps I cheat on a test in school. I do this in order to get a good grade, to win applause, so that I can get a degree from the right school. But precisely because I know I cheated, the grade and the applause and the degree are robbed of whatever meaning and fulfillment they might have had. I cannot live in them; they cannot become part of my house.

Maybe I use manipulation and anger to get what I want from my business associates, my friends, even my family. I know how to get conformity. But to precisely the degree that I use these tools I cannot enter the *intimacy* that I truly desire. I cannot live in these relationships; they cannot become part of my house.

This becomes the truth about me. If I do not know it today, the day is coming when it will be made plain. We all face the storm.

To every student comes examination day. A loving teacher doesn't try to spare the student from this, but rather prepares the student for it. Examination day simply makes apparent what is already reality. No matter how painful it is to face reality, it is never better to hide from it. The day of judgment — the final story — is simply another way of talking about the day when reality will be finally, fully, utterly apparent.

TURNING POINT: WHAT'S THE FOUNDATION?

This brings us to the variable in Jesus' story. Everybody builds a house — both the wise man and the fool, each little piggy. And everybody faces a storm; the wolf knocks at every door.

The question is, what are you going to build your life on? Rock or sand? With what materials — brick or straw? What's the foundation? In what are you placing your ultimate trust?

> To every student comes examination day. A loving teacher doesn't try to spare the student from this, but rather prepares the student for it.

Jesus said that the foolish choice is to build a house on the sand. It is placing your ultimate trust in that which cannot sustain you through the storms of life, gambling that you will get ultimate fulfillment from anything other than life guided by the wisdom and power and care of God.

The man who built on the sand assured his own destruction. The obvious question is, how'd he get into this mess? Notice here that, according to Jesus, he did not deliberately set out to do something evil. Jesus doesn't call him wicked. The adjective Jesus chooses, with surgical precision, is "foolish."

When children do something foolish, their parents, in a futile search for meaning and rationality, always ask the same question.

One word, three letters: "Why?" "Why did you draw on the wall with permanent markers? Why did you place the bike strategically behind the car so it would be backed over and crumpled? Why did you have a contest to see who could stick the longest spaghetti noodle up your brother's nose?"

And children always give the same response: "I don't know." (Apparently this question is part of the final prebirth briefing session: "You'll be asked why a lot. Stick to the standard answer.")

Of course they don't know. If they were operating on the basis of reason and logic, they wouldn't have done it in the first place. "I don't know. It just happened. Seemed like a good idea at the time."

If we were to ask the man in Jesus' story, "Foolish man, why did you build on sand?" what do you think he'd say?

"I don't know. It just happened. Seemed like a good idea at the time."

No one sets out to build on sand. No architect says, "Here's a sandy spot. A good storm would wash a house completely away on this spot. Let's build here."

Life is this way. No one sits down and plans on having a mediocre existence. No couple pledges their troth aiming at getting a divorce someday. Nobody nurses a grudge in hopes of becoming a bitter, resentful person. People don't give birth to children intending to be so busy that their kids won't know them. No one sits down and plans on his life going to hell.

It just happens. Theologian Neal Plantinga writes,

> Sin is both wrong and dumb. Indeed, wherever the follies are playing, sin is the main event. Sin is the world's most impressive *example* of folly. . . . Sin is the wrong recipe for good health; sin is the wrong gasoline to put in the tank; sin is the wrong road to take in order to get home. In other words, sin is finally futile.

Garrison Keillor writes about David Ingqvist, a Lutheran pastor, who despairs at the sheer *folly* of human behavior:

> David glanced at Dear Abby now and then, and it alarmed him how often she recommended ministers. "Talk to your minister," she'd say to the fourteen-year-old girl in love with the fifty-one-year-old auto mechanic (married) who is in prison for rape. Why did Abby assume that a minister could deal with this? The poor old guy is in his study, paging through Revelations, when the door flies open and a teenage girl in a tank top bursts in weeping with passion for an older, married felon three times her age — what is the good reverend to do? Try to interest her in two weeks of handicrafts at Camp Tonawanda?
>
> Poor man. Things were fairly clear to him a moment before, and now, as she pours out her love for Vince, her belief in his innocence, the fact that his wife never loved him, never *really* loved him, not like she, Trish, can love him, and the fact that despite his age and their never having met except in letters there is something indescribably sacred and precious between them, all Pastor can think of is "You're crazy! Don't be ridiculous!" *Thou shalt not be ridiculous.* Paul says, "See then that ye walk circumspectly, not as fools, but as wise, redeeming the time, because the days are evil." How does this apply specifically to Trish, in love by mail . . . ? When Paul wrote that wonderful sentence, he probably was sitting in an upper room in Athens; it was late at night, quiet, and all the fools were asleep. He could write the simple truth, and no fool was around to say, "Huh? What do you mean? Are you saying I *shouldn't* go for the world long-distance walking backward record? But I know I can *do* it! I'm *good* at it! I can walk backward for *miles!*"

Because Jesus loves us, he came as a teacher. He came to offer foolish builders a sure foundation, and careless little pigs a safe place to dwell. He came to teach us how to live. And he says the greatest opportunity we will ever have is to base our life on what he says about God and the world.

For ragged builders like us, each word of Jesus' teaching is a gift of love. And I can receive it one brick at a time:

> For ragged builders like us, each word of Jesus' teaching is a gift of love.

- I confront someone who has hurt me even though I'd rather gossip about him. I know the joy of a restored relationship — or at least the joy of a clean conscience, and I discover that Jesus *really was right*.
- I give money that I would rather hoard. I know the joy of a more generous heart — or at least a heart that's a little less miserly, and I discover that Jesus *really was right*.
- I tell a story simply and truthfully even though I want to shade it to make myself the hero. I know the joy of having been truthful, and I discover that Jesus *really was right*.

I'm building my house with wisdom that I receive one brick at a time.

WHAT HOUSE ARE YOU BUILDING?

One of the strangest houses in the United States is known as the Winchester House, in the Bay area. It was built by Mrs. Winchester, whose husband's wealth came from the rifle associated with their name. Mrs. Winchester lost her husband and her only child, and out of grief or guilt or reasons now lost to time she became obsessed with the occult. She embarked on a massive building project apparently based on the belief that as long as she continued to build her house she would not die.

It is an extraordinary structure. Its construction occupied sixteen carpenters employed full-time for thirty-eight years. At its largest (it has since been partly destroyed by fire), it contained 2,000 doors and 160,000 windows — more windows than the Empire State Building. The front doors were installed at the then-staggering sum of $3,000. They were used only one time — by the men who installed them. There are twists and turns at every hand; secret passageways and hidden corridors and other eccentricities that are harder to fathom: stairs that run to the ceiling and no further, doors that open only into brick walls. All this was done apparently to confuse Death.

She was still building when Death came, and Death was not confused at all. Death has a wonderful sense of direction.

After Mrs. Winchester died, it took eight trucks working full-time every day six and a half weeks to haul away all the building materials and excess junk out of that house. For thirty-eight years they had been coming, and then they came once more. They came for her.

It is an amazing house. But it was built on sand.

Well, little piggy, what's it going to be? Straw or brick? Rock or sand?

Build fast, little piggies, the story goes, your castles in the sand. Make them large and impressive; fill them with wonderful things. But don't forget one thing. Don't forget that the truck will come one day and take it all away. Don't forget that one day Death will come. It will not be confused. It will know just where to look. And it will huff and puff and blow your house down.

Don't forget that the same Jesus who came to be your Savior came also to be your teacher. And he is the wisest human being who ever lived. And so he shared his wisdom with us. He shared it even at the cost of a pain we can't imagine. No one who built a house on a true understanding of Jesus' words has ever been disappointed.

Don't forget that the day is coming when your house, your life, will be tested by God.

And the house on the rock stood firm.

Six

The Contentment
of Being Loved

We are above all things loved — that is the good news of the gospel. . . . To come together as people who believe that just maybe this gospel is actually true should be to come together like people who have just won the Irish sweepstakes.

FREDERICK BUECHNER

A PARABLE OF CONTENTMENT

Once there was a young girl whose parents took her to the Shrine of the Golden Arches. There she saw an opportunity to buy a combination of food and a little toy that someone, in a fit of marketing genius, named the Happy Meal.

"May I have it, please?" she asked her parents. "I must have it. I don't think I could live without it."

"No," her parents told her. "The toy is a trivial little thing that just enabled the price of this package to be raised beyond what it is really worth. It's not in the budget. We can't do it."

But you don't understand, she thought. She knew that they would not just be buying fries, McNuggets, and a dinosaur stamp, they would be buying happiness. She was convinced that she had a little McVacuum at the core of her soul: "Our hearts are restless until they find their rest in a Happy Meal."

So she explained, "I want that Happy Meal more than I've ever wanted anything before. And if I get it, I'll never ask for anything

91

again — ever. No more complaining. No more demanding. If you get me that Happy Meal, I'll be content for the rest of my life."

This seemed like a pretty good deal to her parents, so they bought it.

And it worked.

She grew up to be a contented, grateful, joyful woman. She lived with serenity and grace. Her life in many ways was hard: the man she married turned out to be a louse, and he abandoned her with three small children and no money. The kids too were a disappointment: they dropped out of school, sponged off her meager resources, and eventually left without a trace. When she was an old woman Social Security gave out, and she had to live from hand to mouth.

> Only a child could be foolish enough to believe that a change in circumstance could bring lasting contentment.

But she never complained. She had gotten the Happy Meal. She would think of it often: *I remember that Happy Meal,* she'd say to herself. *What great joy I found there.* Just as she had predicted, it brought her lasting satisfaction. She was grateful the rest of her life.

Does life ever work this way? You would think that after a while children would catch on, that they would say, "You know, a Happy Meal never brings lasting happiness; I'm not going to get suckered into it this time." But it doesn't happen. When the excitement wears off, they need a new fix, another Happy Meal. They keep buying them, and they keep not working. In fact, the only one Happy Meals bring happiness to is McDonald's. Ever wonder why Ronald McDonald wears that grin all the time? Billions of Happy Meals sold.

Of course, only a child would be so naive. Only a child could be foolish enough to believe that a change in circumstance could bring lasting contentment.

Or maybe not. Maybe when you get older, you don't necessarily get any smarter; your Happy Meals just get more expensive.

All day long we are bombarded with messages that seek to persuade us of two things: that we are (or ought to be) discontented and that contentment is only one step away: "use me, buy me, eat me, wear me, try me, drive me, put me in your hair." The things you can buy for hair contentment alone are staggering: You can wash it, condition it, mousse it, dye it, curl it, straighten it, wax it if it's growing where it shouldn't, and Rogaine it if it's not growing where it should.

People are healthier, cleaner, richer, and better informed than ever. We live longer, eat better, dress warmer, work less, and play more than ever in the history of the human race. But are we happier? Or are we just cleaner, healthier, better-coifed discontents? The desperate chase after whatever Happy Meal we were pursuing turns out to have been a trivial pursuit.

THE FRUSTRATION OF TRIVIAL PURSUIT

Years ago when the game first came out, my wife and I spent a frustrating night playing Trivial Pursuit with another couple. Only at rare intervals was someone able to come up with a correct answer. No one was enjoying the game, but we couldn't bring ourselves to stop. Learning theorists say that the hardest behavior to extinguish is behavior that is reinforced on an intermittent schedule. That may explain why Trivial Pursuit was so hard to quit. The most obscure question came when the wife in the other couple asked us, "What color necklace did the Mona Lisa wear?" It happened that my wife had recently seen the painting and remembered Mona Lisa didn't wear any necklace at all! The game had become so aggravating that we were resorting to just making up questions. Nothing is more frustrating than an evening of trivial pursuit.

Unless it is a whole day of trivial pursuit. Nobody wants to get stuck doing trivial things — waiting in line, getting stuck in traffic, performing pointless tasks. Viktor Frankl, the Viennese psychiatrist and survivor of the Holocaust, wrote in his book *Man's Search for Meaning* that one of the most demeaning and even damaging aspects of life in concentration camps was the assignment of deliberately meaningless tasks, such as moving piles of dirt endlessly from one site to another for no purpose at all. I can survive any "how," as long as there is a "why," Frankl wrote.

But it is possible for people to engage in tasks not just for a day, but week after week, year after year, only to conclude they are meaningless. "Vanity of vanities," says the writer of Ecclesiastes. "All is vanity. What do people gain from all the toil at which they toil under the sun? . . . All things are wearisome; more than one can express; the eye is not satisfied with seeing, or the ear filled with hearing." He goes down the list: the pursuit of ultimate pleasure, the attainment of ultimate success, the acquisition of ultimate wealth — none of these is enough to bring lasting satisfaction. The happy wears off. The greatest pursuits end up being trivial. A life of frustration, a whole life devoted to trivial pursuit, is fatal to the human spirit.

Ethicist Richard Mouw was asked by some minister friends to attend a Rolling Stones concert at the Rose Bowl because, they said, they wanted to do some theological reflection on popular culture. So there they were, a group of middle-aged clerics on the Voodoo Lounge tour, calling their teenage children and holding out their cell phones so their kids would hear the Red Hot Chili Peppers warming up the crowd and believe their fathers were really there.

One of the ministers asked Mouw, "There are 85,000 people here; more than will be in all the churches and synagogues of Pasadena this weekend. What would you say to them if you had the chance?"

Mouw had no idea — until Mick Jagger started singing the Stones' signature song, "Satisfaction." Eighty-five thousand people started chanting along: "I can't get no satisfaction. (But I try. . . .)"

Mick Jagger and 85,000 fans had come to the same conclusion as the writer of Ecclesiastes. Great food, great sex, boundless fame, endless wealth, enormous power — these we might be clever enough to attain, but not satisfaction. All these pursuits turn out to be trivial pursuits. A hunger keeps resurfacing that they cannot satisfy.

Why is it that we are so frustrated, so discontent? The amazing answer, in part at least, is that our frustration comes from God himself. Look at these words Paul wrote to Rome: "For the creation was subjected to futility [frustration], not of its own will but by the will of the one who subjected it, in hope that the creation itself will be set free from its bondage to decay and will obtain the freedom of the glory of the children of God."

The picture here is of God "subjecting creation to frustration." God knew that after the Fall we would try to set up other gods, try to give our lives to the pursuit of pleasure or wealth or power or status. So he said that one of the results of the Fall would be that none of these things would be able to bring us "soul satisfaction." Our pursuit of them will always involve a measure of discontent, of disappointment.

But he did this, Paul said, "in hope." God's hope is that we will stop searching for infinite satisfaction from finite objects. His hope is that frustration will once more cause the prodigal son to stop rooting around in the pig trough and return to the father. His hope is that the day will dawn when we realize we "can't get no satisfaction," however hard we try, and come home. Frustration in this sense is a kind of gift. It is one of the forms God's love takes for people who might otherwise throw their lives away on trivial pursuits.

Pursue above all the kingdom of God and his righteousness, Jesus said, and everything else will be thrown in in the bargain. Apart from this, everything else is a trivial pursuit.

New Testament theologian Walter Wink wrote that one of Jesus' most effective teaching techniques was "deliberately-induced frustration." He was forever giving his disciples questions they couldn't answer, assignments they couldn't complete, teaching they couldn't understand. He understood that frustration gets our attention, can open us up to receiving help from beyond ourselves.

GOD'S DISCONTENTED PEOPLE

Discontent was a major theme in the life of Israel from the Exodus onward. For four hundred years the Israelites had been slaves in Egypt. For four hundred years they had dreamed only of liberty; they had known that they would be truly grateful if they could just be free.

Then it happened. God intervened miraculously. Their bondage was over; their enemy was destroyed; they were given identity, security, and the promise of their own homeland. They had everything they wanted. They knew they lived in the loving care of God. They would be grateful forever — right?

> When they came to Marah, they could not drink the water of Marah because it was bitter. . . . And the people *complained* against Moses, saying, "What shall we drink?"

("Complain" and "murmur" will become two of the dominant words in the story of the Exodus. The Greek translation of this word was *gogguzo*, which, like our words "grumble" or "murmur," is what linguists call an onomatopoeia — a word that sounds like what it means. Get a whole crowd of people to chant the word "grumble, grumble, grumble" — it sounds ugly.)

So God intervened again, and miraculously they were given sweet water to drink. Now surely they will be grateful. . . .

A few days later

> the whole congregation of the Israelites complained against Moses and Aaron in the wilderness. The Israelites said to them, "If only we had died by the hand of the LORD in the land of Egypt, when we sat by the fleshpots and ate our fill

of bread; for you have brought us out into this wilderness to kill this whole assembly with hunger."

"If only we had died in Egypt. . . ." These people have raised complaining to a whole new art form. "We're not asking for much — if we just could have had a quick death when our bellies were full. . . . If we just had bread, we'd be grateful forever."

The text mentions three times that "the Lord has heard the complaining" of his people against him. We might expect him to get testy at this point. But he is very patient with his grumbling little rag dolls.

So God intervened again. He rained bread down on them from heaven. It was called manna, which is not a name so much as it is a question. "What is it?" is a loose translation.

Manna was by all accounts an amazing product. It tasted like wafers made with honey. It was apparently a very versatile food. The Israelites were told to bake what they wanted to bake, boil what they wanted to boil, lay aside that which they wanted to eat raw. It sounds a little like Bubba in the movie *Forrest Gump* describing the infinite variety of ways in which you could fix shrimp. "Baked manna, boiled or barbecued manna, manna-on-a-stick, manna burgers, manna-salad, manna-cotti, manna-banana cream pie. . . ."

Now that they had manna they would be grateful, right? No more complaining, right?

At a place called Taberah we're told,

The rabble among them had a strong craving; and the Israelites also wept again, and said, "If only we had meat to eat! We remember the fish we used to eat in Egypt for nothing, the cucumbers, the melons, the leeks, the onions, and the garlic; but now our strength is dried up, and there is nothing at all but this manna to look at."

It was not a Happy Meal anymore.

One of the primary dangers of ingratitude is that it's contagious. Moses couldn't stand it anymore so he took a turn. He speaks to God in words that any self-appointed martyr can identify with:

> One of the primary dangers of ingratitude is that it's contagious.

"Why have you treated your servant so badly? Why have I not found favor in your sight, that you lay the burden of all this people on me? Did I conceive all this people? Did I give birth to them, that you should say to me, 'Carry them in your bosom, as a nurse carries a sucking child, to the land that you promised on oath to their ancestors?' [This would be a rhetorical question.] Where am I to get meat to give to all this people? For they come weeping to me and say, 'Give us meat to eat!' I am not able to carry all this people alone, for they are too heavy for me. If this is the way you are going to treat me, put me to death at once — if I have found favor in your sight — and do not let me see my misery."

Now everybody's asking for Dr. Kevorkian.

When followers give in to this complaining syndrome, it can destroy a leader. When leaders are filled with this darkness, the whole group can lose life. Joy and energy and motivation plummet; everybody wants to quit.

Still God is merciful with his whiners. He will give them exactly what they want: "Consecrate yourselves for tomorrow, and you shall eat meat; for you have wailed in the hearing of the LORD."

But this time there is some judgment mixed in with the mercy. For he will give them *exactly what they want*: "You shall eat not only one day, or two days, or five days, or ten days, or twenty days, but for a whole month — until it comes out of your nostrils and becomes loathsome to you."

The Israelites found that getting what we want will never bring lasting contentment to our discontented lives, and we will come to despise what was once our heart's desire because it did not satisfy.

And so it went for forty years. No matter what God gave them — liberation from slavery, divine guidance, the gift of the Ten Commandments, manna and water, and hope and a future — it was never enough. The people died grumbling.

It is striking to see how destructive the writers of Scripture believe ingratitude is. Paul wrote to the church at Corinth about four activities the people were engaged in during Moses' days: idolatry, sexual immorality, deliberate defiance of God; but the fourth one, the climax of the lot, was "do not complain, as some of them did, and were destroyed by the destroyer."

Ingratitude is one of our most ragged qualities. Art critic Robert Hughes wrote a penetrating critique of American society a few years ago: *The Culture of Complaint.* His thesis is that we live in a society where people perceive themselves to be entitled to having all desires fulfilled. We take this to be part of our birthright. We accord ourselves victim status when it doesn't happen. We live in the culture of complaint. It forms our minds and hearts.

What are the signs that this discontent is present in our lives? Take a moment to do a little inventory.

- I find myself bored or dissatisfied in my work. I expect it not only to pay the bills but to provide me with a sense of identity or significance, and it is crushed beneath the weight of my expectations.
- I am disappointed in my relationships. My friends or spouse or children don't meet all my emotional and intimacy needs, and I find myself growing resentful.
- Rather than losing myself in the moment, I find I get preoccupied in whether or not I am truly happy.
- I try to escape from my discontentment. I seek relief or distraction through watching TV, shopping, or alcohol.

- I lose generosity of spirit. My initial response to events tends to be cynical or even hostile.
- I grow resentful or envious of those whose circumstances seem more pleasant than mine.

John Cheever writes: "The main emotion of the average adult American who has had all the advantages of wealth, education, and culture is *disappointment*." And this is true not only of modern Americans; the human heart has been dissatisfied since we left Eden. But God loves us even with our ragged, insatiable desires. In fact, contentment can only be found in authentic living that is grounded in his love. "You have made us for yourself; and our hearts are restless till they find their rest in Thee," Augustine said.

One option is to do as the Israelites did and grumble through life. Wait for something to make you grateful. Erect your own culture of complaint.

Another way to go would be to keep looking for little happiness fixes that will keep us from noticing our deeper frustration. Psychologist Neil Warren writes: "This headlong pursuit of instantaneous happiness is designed to distract us from the emptiness we feel and to numb the pain of our relational failures and our gnawing sense of futility. This addiction requires daily, sometimes hourly, fixes. . . ."

But God keeps hoping. His hope is that after enough deliberately induced frustration we will finally quit rooting around in the pig trough and come home.

The prophet Isaiah put it like this:

Ho, everyone who thirsts, come to the waters;
and you that have no money, come, buy and eat!
Come, buy wine and milk without money and without
    price.
Why do you spend your money for that which is not bread,
and your labor for that which does not satisfy?

Listen carefully to me, and eat what is good,
and delight yourselves in rich food.

The old translations put it more bluntly: "delight yourself in *fatness*" — the richest, most flavorful portions of meat. No low-fat, low-sodium, soybean-additive meat substitute for Isaiah. The Bible is decidedly pro-fat.

What Isaiah so wants people to know, of course, is that God alone is true bread. Living in his love and care is the only hope for satisfaction of the human heart. "I am the bread of life," he says. "The one who comes to me will never hunger." So God watches in amazement as people wear themselves out pursuing achievements or status or acquisitions which cannot assuage our souls. "Why do you spend your money for that which is not bread?" he asks.

> Living in God's love and care is the only hope for satisfaction of the human heart.

This passage not only contains God's promise to bring contentment, it also points out that people who lack that will inevitably try to distract themselves by seeking temporary happiness wherever they can find it, even though it cannot satisfy their soul. "Why do you spend your money for that which is not bread?" Junk food for the soul. Trivial pursuits. Happy Meals.

Why do you wear yourself out in work, seeking from promotions and achievements what they cannot give?

Why do you devote the hours of your night to endless channel surfing in search of a program about life that can make you laugh, or fear, or simply feel, instead of choosing to live?

Why do you drive yourself into debt seeking to acquire that which money cannot buy?

Of course, achievement and possessions and entertainment are not bad things. They can be very good gifts. But they make very bad gods. They are not enough to build a life on. They cannot nurture the human spirit. They're not bread.

On a plane a few years ago I met a man whose workaholism funded his wife's shopaholic patterns. In fact, he once got a call from an upscale department store she frequented: she had not been there for a week, and they wondered if something was wrong. They kept closer tabs on his wife than he did! He was divorcing his wife and already deeply involved with another woman. Our whole flight together was a litany of his complaints.

People sometimes wonder, *If God wants me to be grateful, why doesn't he just give me everything I want?*

Wise parents know that the most certain way to raise an ungrateful child is to give her everything she wants.

Last Halloween a friend of mine answered one doorbell to find a full-grown woman trick-or-treating. "It's for my daughter," she apologized. It was a little on the chilly side, so the mom decided to drive her daughter around the neighborhood rather than make her put on a coat. And her daughter got so comfortable in the car she fell asleep, so rather than wake her up the mom was going door to door getting the candy. The only thing left was for the mom to binge on the candy and thus spare her daughter the stomachache. The English playwright J. M. Barrie was at the home of a couple he knew when the woman said to her young son, "Stop eating that candy, or you'll be sick tomorrow." "No," said the boy, as he calmly went on eating, "I shall be sick tonite." Barrie was so struck by the exchange that he put it in his play, *Peter Pan*. What happened to the boy remains a mystery.

Oddly enough, people who constantly have every appetite gratified from childhood on become the least capable of gratitude. To become grateful, I must learn that I can handle disappointment and delayed gratification with grace and perseverance. This is why practices such as fasting and simplicity are such powerful tools for transformation. *The experience of frustration and disappointment is irreplaceable in the development of a grateful heart.*

THAT WHICH IS BREAD: THE CONTENTMENT OF BEING LOVED

Some time ago I had a day of solitude in a forest preserve. I felt the kind of "weariness of the flesh" the writer of Ecclesiastes talked about. And I realized how strongly I had been living for certain achievements, and how I felt it as heaviness when they were not realized. I was caught up in my own trivial pursuits.

But I was in the kind of natural setting where it is hard to remain discontent for long. The chestnut trees and oaks and maples and sycamores were on fire with autumn colors in brilliant October sunshine. And something happened. I began to get free. I was somehow given the gift of sensing that God loved me. I began to feel again what a gift it was to be alive, on *this* earth, in *this* place, during *this* moment. I was immersed in this sense so strongly I began to run, just in the strength of that feeling.

> I began to get free. I was somehow given the gift of sensing that God loved me.

Richard Foster wrote once of a father walking through a mall with his two-year-old son. The child was cranky; he kept whining and wriggling and complaining. The father struggled to remain patient.

Usually stories like this don't have happy endings. In another one, a father with an out-of-control two-year-old is walking through a grocery store, repeating in a calm voice, "It's okay, Danny. You can do this, Danny. We're almost done, Danny."

Somebody asked him, "Is your son Danny having a bad day?"

"My son's name is Nathan," the man said. "*My* name is Danny."

But the father that Richard Foster writes about adopts another strategy. He scooped up his little two-year-old grumbler, held him tight to his chest, and began to sing an impromptu love song. None of the words rhymed. He sang it off-key, but as best as he could, he shared his heart: "I love you. I'm so glad you're my boy. You make me laugh."

From store to store the father kept going, words not rhyming, notes off-key. His son relaxed, captivated by this strange and wonderful song.

Finally, when they had finished, the dad went to the car, buckled his son in the car seat, and his son raised his arms and lifted up his head. "Sing it to me again, Daddy. Sing it to me again."

Somehow when I was alone with his creation on that day in the forest, God sang that song to me. It didn't matter who I was or what I'd done, being alive and loved by God was enough to bring gratitude and contentment — at least for a few moments.

Yet that wonderful feeling didn't completely fade away, even after I'd left the forest.

Several days later, I was sitting in a meeting, and suddenly I was aware that I didn't have to say anything. Often I would want to speak, not necessarily because I had something to contribute, but simply to let people know I had an idea or that I had read something, or I'd want to say something to make them think I was smart or could win an argument.

But this time, sitting there in the meeting, I carried that time alone in the forest preserve with me. God loved me.

This awareness that God gave me is hard to describe: there was a kind of lightness of being in my soul in that moment. I could talk — if I had something worth saying. But I didn't need to. I didn't need to try to show I had power. I didn't need to manage impressions. I had better food than that to eat. I was content.

I tasted, at least I think a little bit, what the psalmist meant: "The Lord is my shepherd; I shall not want." I had been led beside still waters and green pastures.

I just sat there, part of me listening to conversation, part of me saying, "Sing it again, Daddy. Tell me you love me, God."

PRACTICING GRATITUDE

Lewis Smedes writes that when the Bible says we ought to be grateful, it is not so much the ought of obligation as it is an ought of opportunity. When the primary motive of gratitude is obligation, it tends to choke out the heart.

Parents have a question they ask of children. Every generation of parents has asked it after someone gives their child a gift or does them a favor: "What do you say?"

"What do you say to the nice man?" "What do you say to Aunt Eva for her Velveeta, Spam, and lima bean casserole?" my parents would ask me.

How's a kid supposed to respond?

It was not really a question. They'd

> When the primary motive of gratitude is obligation, it tends to choke out the heart.

have been surprised if I'd said, "Aunt Eva, what in the name of heaven were you thinking? Aunt Eva, you should not be allowed to prepare meals — someone should put you away."

"What do you say?" Thank you.

The question may elicit the words, but the response is usually pretty mechanical.

My parents would also have been surprised at genuine emotion. "Aunt Eva, I have a sense of awe and wonder at what I've just experienced. I am but a child. Without an adult providing for me as you have done I would die. You've presented this meal freely, as an act of love and service for me. Aunt Eva, you are a humanitarian, and in the name of children everywhere I salute you."

No, generally I gave a minimalist response: "Thank you."

Even if children don't *feel* gratitude, we want them to learn to offer thanks simply as a matter of civility. Even if my heart doesn't feel it, I need to offer thanks simply because doing so is right — I owe a debt of gratitude.

But our hope is that our children won't just parrot the words. Our hope is that one day they will become grateful persons, because the ability to experience gratitude and offer heartfelt praise and thanksgiving is one of the most fundamental signs of life and spiritual wholeness.

"Let me live that I may praise you," the psalmist says to God. True gratitude means coming to see that everything is a gift, and life the greatest gift of all.

G. K. Chesterton once said, "Here ends another day during which I have had eyes, ears, hands, and the great world around me, and tomorrow begins another. Why am I allowed two?"

Life is good. Life is a gift.

Almost eight years ago, Nancy and I were in the delivery room for the birth of our final child, first son. She was delivering, I was coaching. (That was our role the first two times around, and it worked out pretty well.)

Everything seemed to be going on schedule. Nancy was declaring in no uncertain terms that the pain was unbearable and that she would get even with me one day for doing this to her, but this was the drill in previous births, so I thought things were okay.

Then the doctor's eyes got very serious. He gave several instructions, reached for some kind of instrument, and the situation became very urgent. We didn't know it at the time, but the baby's umbilical cord was wrapped around his neck, his face was blue; he could have strangled if the situation were not handled carefully.

The doctor was struggling as Nancy was writhing in pain. He got the baby far enough out that he could reach down and cut the umbilical cord. By now blood was spurting everywhere, the baby and Nancy were crying, but the doctor smiled: "Everything's going to be okay."

Maybe so, but by this time I was getting dizzy. "I've got to sit down." I slumped to a chair, and the doctor told me to put my head between my legs.

Nancy asked, "Are you sure everything will be okay?"

"Yes," the doctor said. "In fact your son and your husband are pinking up at just about the same time."

And I knew, in that moment, that I had received a gift, that all the earth is a gift, and life is the most precious gift. It is not a right. It can't be taken for granted. It can be snuffed out in a second. Life is a gift. And it is good. It is so good to be alive. I was as grateful as I've ever been in my life.

> Learning to live in the contentment of being loved means receiving the gift of perspective.

Learning to live in the contentment of being loved means receiving the gift of perspective. So much of the way I feel about my life depends on the perspective from which I view it. A friend told me about a letter a college student wrote to her parents:

Dear Mom and Dad,

I have so much to tell you. Because of the fire in my dorm set off by the student riots, I experienced temporary lung damage and had to go to the hospital. While I was there, I fell in love with an orderly, and we have moved in together. I dropped out of school when I found out I was pregnant, and he got fired because of his drinking, so we're going to move to Alaska, where we might get married after the birth of the baby.

Signed,
Your loving daughter

P.S.: None of that really happened, but I did flunk my chemistry class and I wanted you to keep it in perspective.

GRATITUDE FOR WHAT I HAVE

When I believe a change in my circumstances — say a new car — would make me grateful, here's what that way of thinking really amounts to. I list some of the truly wonderful things I already have:

- I was made in the image of God. I have a body, and most of it works. I have eyes that see and feet that walk. Many people don't. Yet that's what I have each day.
- God loves me. He calls me his child. Because Jesus came to teach and live, died on a cross and was resurrected — I have a future assured with God forever.
- I have been received into God's ultimate dream: the new community. I'm part of the church. I belong — I can be loved and accepted.
- I have been gifted, created to make a unique, eternal contribution to the work of God. I have a calling. Even when I foul up, God promises to work through me in spite of my mistakes.

When I complete this inspiring list, I conclude that all these gifts combined — the gift of life, a body that works, being a child of God, having assurance of God's love through Christ, royal priesthood in the church, the guidance and power of the Holy Spirit in my life — are not enough to produce lasting gratitude. But, I say to myself, if I had all this *and a really cool car*, then I'd be grateful forever.

LEARN TO DELIGHT IN IMPERFECT GIFTS

Ever go to one of those outlet stores where they sell products labeled "slightly imperfect"? Sometimes the imperfections are easily seen, other times they are barely noticeable. The same is true in our lives, not only with the products we buy, but with the gifts we receive.

If you're married, it didn't take you long to realize that your spouse was a "slightly imperfect" gift. Undoubtedly your spouse has noted the same thing about you.

When children are born, we often exclaim, "She's perfect!" Well, you and I both know that it doesn't take long to realize that the possession of ten fingers and ten toes does not constitute perfection. Your children could probably vouch for the fact that there aren't too many perfect parents in this world, either.

On the material side, which one of us hasn't received a holiday gift that we later returned because it was the wrong color or size?

What about our bodies? We go through life thinking, *If my body were different, if it were perfect, if I had someone else's, then I'd be grateful.* Your body may not be perfect, but it's a pretty helpful thing to have.

I must learn to be grateful for all the "slightly imperfect" gifts in my life. If I withhold my gratitude in hopes of receiving the perfect spouse, child, body, or birthday present, I will never be grateful at all.

God himself chooses to delight in imperfect gifts — in you and me. Even though our hearts are flawed and shadowed, even though we give them tentatively and with mixed motives, he receives them with unspeakable joy. Heaven itself rejoices at the gift of one repentant sinner's heart.

Yet God knows what it is to have his gifts — perfect in their original form — cast aside as if they were "slightly imperfect." His creation has been misused, his words misquoted, his purposes mocked. Jesus, who once spoke worlds into being, knew the frustration of presenting the gift of his words to people who refused to hear them. He knew the frustration of longing to impart the gift of forgiveness to people who refused to repent, longing to grant healing to people who refused to believe, longing to give community and gather together like a mother hen little chicks who refused to be gathered. Jesus knew the frustration of throwing a banquet to which guests refused to come, pouring wine they would not drink, bringing bread they would not eat.

And at the end he knew the frustration of the cross. What he knew to be the ultimate gift the world made into the ultimate attempt to thwart the will and work of God.

But Jesus' frustration was bathed in hope. For the cross which was meant to frustrate the purpose of God became its final expression and guarantee.

For the miracle of God's love for ragged people is that in a whole universe that obeyed his will, in a cosmos of beauty and order, his concern should extend to one crooked little planet in one insignificant corner of one small galaxy in the whole of his work. It would be easier for him just to erase it. One rebel planet seems too small to be worth his time to run after, seems like a trivial pursuit.

The miracle of God's love is that he should become a human being and work as a carpenter and grow hungry and tired and weak and should teach and even cry for you and me. For in the end, the story of God's love for this world is the story of a pursuit that is trivial no longer. Not after God became man. Not after the cross.

SEVEN

THE ROUNDABOUT WAY

*The man who does not permit his spirit to be beaten down
and upset by dryness and helplessness, but who lets God lead
him peacefully through the wilderness, and desires no other
support or guidance than that of pure faith and trust in God
alone, will be brought to the Promised Land.*

THOMAS MERTON

When you're going on a journey and have small children with
you, there is one question that you will inevitably face. The
children will ask it. They will ask it soon, they will ask it often,
they will ask it with a kind of whining, obstinate passion. They
will ask it even though you warn them you never want to hear it
again. They will ask it as though they have a legal obligation to do
so. It will irritate you — like fingernails scraping a blackboard — as
it is designed to do.

"Are we there yet?"

Generally there is an inverse correlation between how long the
trip will be and how quickly the question begins. It's only a matter
of time before someone in the backseat complains about being
pushed or punched or psychologically harassed. Boundaries are
marked, and then someone's airspace gets violated. Before long, it
gets set to music, like some kind of pagan chant, *Are we there yet?
Are we there yet?*

Imagine going on a trip and saying, "We're not there yet. We
won't get there today. We won't get there tomorrow. In fact, our

whole life is going to be a journey. We are headed for the one destination in the world worth traveling to, and we have wonderful assurances about our ultimate arrival — but not yet."

THE GOD OF THE ROUNDABOUT WAY

The children of God were getting ready to go on a journey. They were going from slavery to freedom; from poverty to abundance; to the Promised Land, a place flowing with milk and honey.

It sounded like a very simple journey. There were only two parts to the journey as God described it to Moses. I will "bring them up out of that land," God said, referring to Egypt and hunger and slavery, "to a good and broad land, a land flowing with milk and honey." "Out of" one land and "to" another.

They could not have expected it would take long. Once they left Egypt, all they had to do was to cross the Sinai peninsula. It was not a terribly long trip — less than 200 miles. They could do it in a matter of weeks.

But God had an alternate route in mind.

The Bible says, "When Pharaoh let the people go, God did not lead them by way of the land of the Philistines, although that was nearer; for God thought, 'If the people face war, they may change their minds and return to Egypt.' So God led the people by the roundabout way of the wilderness."

This is the God who, precisely because he loves his children, refuses to take the shortcut they would much prefer. Because of their lack of faith, their fear, he sends them on the roundabout way. Later on, of course, because of their rebellion and sin, the way would become more roundabout still. This is what Pastor David Handley called the roundabout ways of God.

Are we there yet?

Not yet. One day, but not yet. Be patient.

Imagine: the whole nation gathers, and the day they have awaited for four hundred years dawns. They are setting out on their journey home. None of them have been there yet, but they're not worried about directions. There is a pillar of cloud and fire in front of them. The fire that burned in the bush for Moses now burns for them all. They will be guided by God.

The pillar starts to move and the march begins. But then the people notice the pillar is going the wrong way! The Promised Land is northeast, and the pillar's headed south. The pillar is directionally challenged.

Are we there yet? the people wonder.

What can Moses say? His directions were not very precise. This was the only time in history when a wife said to her husband, "Do you know where you're going? Are we going the right way?" and the husband responded, "God only knows," that he was speaking simple literal truth.

Will the people follow God even when they don't understand? Will they follow him when following doesn't seem to make any sense? Will they stay faithful on the roundabout way of God?

God does lead his people on roundabout ways. He does not move hastily. He is never in a hurry. It is one of his most irritating qualities.

Richard Mouw writes that in our day we need theological correction under the general heading "Your God is too fast." God can of course move quickly. He can answer prayer dramatically, in the twinkling of an eye, to use St. Paul's phrase. But as a general rule he is remarkably patient. The Mennonites have a saying, "We are living in the time of God's patience." God is delaying the end of history out of love, so that as many human beings as possible may seek him and be saved.

He is the God who takes his people to the Promised Land by way of the desert. He is the God of the roundabout way.

THE DESERT EXPERIENCE

For Israel this would not be just a minor detour. They would spend forty years on this roundabout way. Forty years in the desert.

Forty is a significant number in Scripture. Old Testament scholars tell us it was used as a round number to designate a fairly long period of time in terms of human existence or endurance. Forty years was the span of a generation. Isaac and Esau married at forty; David and Solomon reigned forty years. Forty days marked the time of the flood, the time Moses spent on Mount Sinai, and the period between Jesus' resurrection and ascension.

But the number forty is associated with the desert especially. When Moses killed an Egyptian and fled from Pharaoh, he lived in the Midian desert forty years. When Elijah ran in fear from Jezebel, he was led into the wilderness on a journey of forty days and forty nights. And, of course, Jesus himself began his ministry with forty days of fasting and prayer in the desert.

Over and over it happens in the lives of those who seek God. Everybody is going to log some time in the desert. Life begins at forty.

The desert is the place where you did not want to go. It is not flowing with milk and honey. It is a dry and barren place. Life is bleak there.

If you take faith in God seriously you too will learn something of his roundabout ways. You will know times when your heart aches with hurt or loss. Times when you are fatigued and even sleep does not refresh you. Times when you long for a good thing, when your motives seem pure, when it seems like God could so easily answer your prayer, yet he does not. Times when life hardly seems worth the effort.

Often the journey to the desert is triggered by some event. A relationships shatters. A child rebels, a prodigal son or daughter leaves your home and does not come back. You endure a financial disaster. You cherish a dream for years, looking forward to the day when it is going to come true, and then one day you realize not only has it not come true so far, but it is not going to happen. The dream dies, and so do you.

But sometimes the desert seems to come for no discernible reason at all.

In these times, even faith is hard. You pray, you pour your heart out to God, but there is no response. No sense of nearness. The Bible is no comfort. You are confused, and you wonder why, but you receive no answer. It is your spirit, your soul, that feels dry and barren. You are not just in the desert. The desert is in you.

> God's way is rarely the quickest way. It is seldom the easiest way. But it is always the best way.

In the desert all we have to cling to is the promise.

God has not forgotten you. You have not been abandoned. He leads his children in roundabout ways. He is not in a hurry.

God is at work in the roundabout way of the desert, in ways we do not see and cannot understand. God's way is rarely the quickest way. It is seldom the easiest way. But it is always the best way.

THE DESERT EARLY IN THE CHRISTIAN LIFE

John of the Cross wrote that a desert experience, or what he calls the dark night of the soul, is often a part of a believer's experience not long after conversion. It is, he said, a necessary part of growth.

Here's how it often happens. When you first become a Christian, God often gives a gift of pure spiritual desire. You have a ravenous appetite to know more about God. You find yourself longing to pray. You're hungry to read the Bible, and it feels as if God is talking directly to you through it. Worship is alive for you. Your heart fills up — you can hardly find words to express thoughts and feelings. You find yourself not wanting to sin. Things that used to tempt you just seem to have lost their hold on you. Your heart is tender toward God and people. You find yourself wanting to go around doing random acts of kindness toward people.

It may be, if you're lucky, that you go on like this for fifty or sixty years, then die. It may be that your whole life will have been a straight line of spiritual growth.

But for most of us, life does not work that way. For most of us, somewhere along the line things change. What was once easy and simple and enjoyable has now become laborious and draining. You find yourself not wanting to pray. You pray less often, and when you do, you miss that old sense of excitement. It is difficult to sense God's presence. The Bible feels dull. You find yourself troubled by doubts and confusion. Temptations that you thought you had overcome begin to look good again. Sometimes when you are in worship, other people are deeply moved — to tears maybe — but for you the tears don't come.

Have you ever gone through anything like this?

You are experiencing spiritual dryness. It *may* be the result of deliberate, ongoing sin. If so, you need to confess and repent. But often, it seems to come out of the blue. You don't want to feel this way.

You wonder, *Why does God allow this to happen? Why can't it always be as easy as it was at first? Why the roundabout road?*

Something very important is happening. It is a part of growing up. A parable may help here.

My first real bike was a red English racer. I wanted to learn to ride that bike more than anything in the world. One day my dad took the training wheels off. I wasn't quite ready to solo, so my dad held the back of the bicycle with one hand and ran alongside me. I felt like I was a pro, but the truth, of course, was that he was behind me propping me up. I couldn't really ride yet.

Then one day he did a strange thing. He let go.

That was a dirty trick, I thought, because I fell. Hard.

And he kept letting go, and I kept falling. It got so bad my mother pulled the curtains closed because she couldn't stand to watch. Apparently either the bike was lopsided or I was.

"Dad, how come you can't keep holding on?"

"Because if I do you'll never learn how," he said. "You'll never ride on your own. Do you want to be twenty-five years old and still have me running behind you holding up your bike?"

"Yes," I said. It sounded preferable to what was going on. But in retrospect, I see his wisdom.

He hadn't abandoned me. It was a roundabout way of learning to ride a bike, but there was no other.

When first you ride on your own, unsupported, you feel like you're doing worse than ever. You're falling all over the place. The fact is, you're growing. You just don't know it.

C. S. Lewis wrote that when in the first days of spiritual life God gives us freedom from temptation and the desire to pray, he is making it easy for us. And we're tempted to think, *It's all me! I have reached spiritual gianthood already.*

Lewis went on to say,

> But God never allows this state of affairs to last long. Sooner or later he withdraws, if not in fact, at least from their obvious experience, all those supports and incentives. He leaves the creature to stand up on its own legs — to carry out from the will alone duties which have lost all relish. It is during such trough periods, much more than during peak periods, that it is growing into the sort of creature he wants it to be. Hence the prayers offered in the state of dryness are those which please him best.

Perhaps you are at a place where you don't feel the hand of God. You may not have felt it for some time. You're tempted to give up. But the truth is you've got a chance to learn how to ride.

THE DESERT AS A PLACE OF STRENGTHENING

Why does God take the Israelites on the scenic route? The Bible says the reason is that God knows that if they go the direct route, if they face opposition, "they may change their minds and return to Egypt."

The direct route, the Sinai interstate, would take them past people who were hostile to them. God was perfectly capable of delivering them, but they did not believe that yet. They were too frightened.

Someone once said, "It took one night to get Israel out of Egypt. It took forty years to get Egypt out of Israel." For four hundred years the Israelites had been slaves, and they thought of themselves as slaves still. So God would have to take some time to develop the courage and faith of his people.

> When you can give thanks in the desert, you grow very strong.

It's easy to trust in the land of milk and honey when everything's working out right. When prayers get answered and problems go away and the kids' teeth are straight and your boss likes you, faith is not hard. But the desert has a way of building strength. God is not nearly as concerned with *where* his people are going as *who they will be* when they get there.

Joseph is promised that he will be a great leader. Next thing he knows, he is sold into slavery and ends up in an Egyptian jail for years. He dies without ever making it to the Promised Land. In fact, we're told that Moses carried Joseph's bones out of Egypt. Joseph knew the roundabout way.

David was anointed king of Israel. Soon after that, he found himself a homeless fugitive living in caves to escape being killed by a hostile king. David knew the roundabout way.

Daniel was gifted, wise, and faithful. He ended up in exile in a strange land, thrown into a den of lions. God was still leading Daniel, but he was leading him on a roundabout way.

When you can give thanks in the desert, you grow very strong. When you are on the roundabout way but say, "I won't go back to Egypt. I will be faithful," you are growing mighty in your soul.

Perhaps you would like to be in a relationship; you're looking for a life partner, seeking a good thing. But you have been on a roundabout way. You have been waiting for Mr. or Ms. Right and you have been waiting a long time. You're tempted to think, *Maybe I'll settle for Mr. Not-so-terribly-wrong.*

Will you follow Christ then? Completely? Will you make the following commitments? "I will not get entangled in a romantic relationship with someone who does not share my faith and ultimate values. I will not get sexually involved with a person to whom I am not married — even in the face of great pressure. If I have to stop the relationship I will. Now. I am going to stay on the roundabout way of the Lord. If it means forty years, I will endure forty years. If it's the rest of my life, I will stay the rest of my life."

THE DESERT AS THE PLACE OF ENDURANCE

It would be nice if the desert were a one-time-only experience, like getting vaccinated or having your wisdom teeth pulled. But the desert is a place we return to again and again. It comes when we are lonely or tired or tempted.

Perhaps you are considering a relationship that you know would be destructive to you and would dishonor God, but you're lonely or afraid, or you're just tired of holding out.

Perhaps you have a difficult person in your life: a parent, a child, or a coworker. You don't know how to redeem this relationship. You are at the end of your resources.

Perhaps you wrestle over and over with the same sin. You try to grow but continually fall back. You've confessed, resolved, nothing seems to work. You are ready to secretly resign yourself to never overcoming it.

The desert is the place of temptation. It was in the desert that Jesus faced the temptation to turn aside from doing the will of his Father, to take a shortcut to ruling the kingdoms of the world rather than the roundabout way of the cross. The desert is where you face the question of perseverance. The desert is a place where only the patient can go on. Will you follow the pillar again today? Will you continue to follow when all outside support to following is gone?

Perhaps your marriage has become a desert experience. You had hopes and dreams for it that haven't come true, may never come true. Will you be patiently obedient to God in your marriage? Will you love your spouse one day at a time? Will you love as wisely as you can, love when the props of romance or bubbling hormones or easy compatibility are kicked out from under you?

An elderly couple lies in bed. She is not satisfied with the distance between them. She reminds him, "When we were young, you used to hold my hand in bed."

He hesitates, but in a few moments a wrinkled hand snakes across the bed and grasps hers. She is not satisfied.

"When we were young, you used to cuddle right up next to me."

More serious hesitation now. But eventually, with a few groans, he laboriously turns his body and cradles hers as best he can.

She is not satisfied.

"When we were young, you used to nibble on my ear."

Loud sigh. He throws back the covers and bolts out of bed. She is somewhat hurt by this.

"Where are you going?"

"To get my teeth."

It's one thing to nibble on an ear when you're young and in love and the air is filled with the scent of eau de something-or-other and nibbling is easy.

It's another thing to nibble when the ear doesn't hear so well anymore and contains a hearing device, and the air is filled with the scent of Ben Gay, and you have to go get your teeth first.

The desert is the place where you learn to obey when obeying is no longer easy. Therefore, it can be the place of great strengthening.

THE DESERT IS THE PLACE OF GOD'S LOVE

Odd as it sounds, the desert can offer a unique opportunity to experience the depth of God's love.

When you're at the top of your game — praying with fierce joy, untroubled by temptation, triumphing in ministry, and you come to God and hear again the message that he loves you, it is a great thing.

In the desert, though, the word of God's love can speak to a deeper place in your heart. In the desert you come to God and you haven't prayed well (or maybe at all), you have been battered by temptation, rocked by doubts, and feel you may be more hindrance than help to whatever work God may be doing in the world. Yet even so you hear the words, "I still love you. I could not love you more than I do now. I still want you for my child. Haven't you learned? You are the object of my undying affection. You are the beloved."

> The desert can offer a unique opportunity to experience the depth of God's love.

To be loved when we are feeling lovable — that's good. To be loved when we are feeling unlovely, unlovable — that's life to someone who's dying. That's grace.

The desert is the place where I can learn to live for the love of God.

Some time ago at a restaurant, one of our children found a coin-operated machine that featured a crane which, if operated just right, could retrieve a toy for the skilled operator. It cost fifty cents a pop. At first our child loved that machine. But it took every cent she had and never yielded a thing. It bled her dry. Then she didn't love it anymore.

Desert times are those times when I don't get the promotion, house, success, reputation, or even the health I wanted. Then I find out whether I love God for God's sake, or simply because he gives me milk and honey. What do I do when I keep putting prayers in the coin slot but nothing comes out?

The desert really was intended to be a place where God could be present with his people so they could come to know and trust him. Brevard Childs writes, "God's plan was that they should learn to love him in the wilderness and that they should always look back upon the time in the desert as the idyllic time of their life with him alone."

Of course the desert was not the Promised Land. Life there was not easy. Forty years there was an expression of judgment, the result of sin. But even God's judgment is filled with love, and God's ultimate desire for Israel was that the desert be not a place of pain but of love.

In the desert there were no great cities to build. No great battles to win. Just God and his rag dolls. He would feed them every morning, guide them every day, and protect them every night. The desert was intended by God to be life beyond achievement. It was to be a life of love.

Frederick Buechner writes of how the desert can be the place of God's love:

> When the worst happens, or almost happens, a kind of peace comes. I had passed beyond grief, beyond terror, all but beyond hope, and it was there, in that wilderness, that for the first time in my life I caught sight of something of what it must be like to love God truly. It was only a glimpse, but it was like stumbling on fresh water in the desert . . . I loved him because there was nothing else left. I loved him because he seemed to have made himself as helpless in his might as I was in my helplessness. I loved him not so much in spite of there being nothing in it for me but almost because there was nothing in it for me. For the first time in my life, there in that wilderness, I caught what it must be like to love God truly, for his own sake, to love him no matter what.

HOPE ON THE ROUNDABOUT WAY

Sandy's life had been a pleasant path. She was raised in the faith; her grandfather was the pastor of the church where she grew up. She graduated from a Christian college, began to work as a pediatric nurse, and married a fine Christian young man.

Four years later, two months pregnant with her first child, her husband told her he felt trapped and wasn't sure he was ready for parenthood. Two months later she became quite ill, and while she was staying at her sister's, he left.

Sandy didn't know it, but she had stepped onto the roundabout way. She kept praying for her husband, certain that he would return like the prodigal son. But she found out her husband had been unfaithful. Not only that, but he had contracted a sexually transmitted disease.

When the baby was born, her father's gift to her was the disease that he had passed on. At the moment of delivery her baby was silent when she should have cried, blue and limp when she should have been pink and wriggling. Rachel was born anacephalic, with only a brain stem to carry on the most basic functions.

The doctors said she would live only a matter of days or weeks, but the weeks became months and the months became years. Sandy's whole life consisted of working twelve-hour shifts while her sister or a friend was with the baby, then spending the rest of the day caring for Rachel.

This roundabout way was paved with none of the dreams parents usually have for their children. Sandy would never videotape Rachel toddling off to her first day of school; there would be no report cards, no homemade valentines, no baking cookies together, no driver's license test, no walk down the aisle. Sandy would never see her daughter take her first step, never feel chubby little fingers grasp her hand, never hear her laugh or say the phrase "I love you" or even the syllables "Mommy."

Sandy could never even tell if Rachel knew who her mother was. The only time Rachel seemed to respond to anything at all was at times during her baths: Sandy would wash and rub her back, and Rachel would sometimes make a low cooing sound, as if she were content.

One day Sandy decided to take a vacation, her first in three years. It would be the first day she had spent apart from Rachel since she was born. When Sandy called from her hotel, her sister held the phone up to Rachel's ear and then told Sandy that Rachel had cooed at the sound of her voice. It was the only indication Sandy ever had that perhaps her daughter knew her.

When she landed at the airport, her brother-in-law met her with the words that somehow she knew were coming: Rachel had died.

Rachel's father never came to the funeral, never asked about his daughter, never said, "I'm sorry." It was not until six years later that Sandy could read the journals she kept during Rachel's life. Mostly they were asking why. "There were no answers then," Sandy said. "I have none now." It is a dark road, this roundabout way.

And yet, ask Sandy if she would prefer that Rachel had never been born, and she would tell you that is unthinkable. She speaks of experiencing a communion while holding that baby that was deeper than words can say. She speaks of learning what it means to love beyond all limitations and imperfections, to see right down into the spirit and love that. She has no regrets about bringing Rachel home and lavishing love on her.

She speaks of choosing forgiveness. She had to forgive a husband who never asked for forgiveness, never seemed to want it, certainly never deserved it. She had to forgive him because the alternative was life in the prison of resentment.

She had to forgive herself, for the bitterness and the darkness and the limitations and the choices that she wished she could have back.

And in a strange way, she had to do something like forgive God, for not answering honest prayer, for not protecting Rachel.

Somehow on the roundabout way, though there may be questions that don't get answered and confusion that does not lift, still one must choose. Is there hope on this roundabout way? Is it a cul-de-sac, or does it lead finally, after all the twists and turns, to home?

A CATASTROPHE THAT MIGHT BECOME A STORY

Norman MacLean has a beautiful passage in his haunting book Young Men and Fire. It is the poetic story of his painstaking, four-decades-long attempt to find meaning in the deaths of a squadron of young Smoke-jumpers (airborne firefighters) in a fire in the Mann Gulch Montana wilderness in 1948. It is also a meditation on life and mortality made more urgent by the death of his own wife.

MacLean writes of the Mann Gulch deaths:

> This is a catastrophe that we hope will not end where it began; it might go on and become a story. . . . [We hope] that in this cockeyed world there are shapes and designs, if only we have some curiosity, training, and compassion and take care not to lie or be sentimental . . . then what we would be talking about would start to change from catastrophe without a filled-in story to what could be called the story of a tragedy, but tragedy would be only a part of it, as it is of life.

Catastrophe is not only brutal, it is randomly brutal. There is nothing personal about it. It is an accident. It is the chance grinding of the unfeeling gears of a cosmic machine. It has no meaning, no significance, only pain. If human existence is merely a catastrophe — a roll of the dice that will one day end when the last life is snuffed out — then we are without hope. In catastrophe, the cry of dereliction is the last word.

But a story has meaning. Where there is story, there is a Storyteller. Stories may involve tragedy, but tragedies are personal; they have significance. And therefore, where there is tragedy, there is the possibility of redemption. Where there is tragedy, there is hope.

The writers of Scripture knew all about catastrophe. The human race has been familiar with it since the Fall. But God is determined that the human race will not end in catastrophe, that it will go on and become a story. Christian hope is based on the proclamation that God chose to take our tragedy on himself. God himself walked the roundabout way. MacLean writes,

> Where there is tragedy, there is the possibility of redemption. Where there is tragedy, there is hope.

The most eloquent expression of this cry was made by a young man who came from the sky and returned to it and who, while on earth, knew he was alone and beyond all other men, and who, when he died, died on a hill: "About the ninth hour he cried with a loud voice, 'Eli, Eli, lama sabach-thani?'" ("My God, my God, why has thou forsaken me?").

Christian hope says that God himself walked the Via Dolorosa — the roundabout way. Therefore the cross is not just a catastrophe — it is on its way to becoming a story. And the day is coming when it will redeem your story and mine, if we'll let it.

Christian hope says the Cry of Dereliction is a real word, but it is not to be the last word.

Christian hope says that what happened to Sandy is not just catastrophe. It is not merely some faulty genetic accident, a bit of bad DNA, which consigns Rachel to being a brief meaningless accident in the cosmic scheme of things. Christian hope says that what happened to Sandy and Rachel is part of a story, a tragic story so far, but tragedy is not the whole of it. Christian hope says that flawed DNA will not be allowed to take the last hand. Christian hope says that one day Sandy and Rachel will be seated at a table where they will each know each other and be fully known; and the words of wonder and gratitude and love that Rachel could not speak here will flow ceaselessly there; and the limbs that hung limp and useless in this world will define grace and beauty in that one; the mind that was cheated here will flourish in endless creativity and sparkling intelligence. Christian hope says the One who does reconstructive surgery is not yet finished, and that the day will come when a short-lived, little-noticed rag doll in this world will dazzle through the ages with a glory that we cannot now imagine or comprehend.

Christian hope says we are on our way from catastrophe to tragedy to a story of glory. We are on our way. It may be a ragged way, a roundabout way, but it's bound for glory nevertheless.

Are we there yet?

Not yet. One day, but not yet. Be patient.

Eight

Love and Grace

Now we have received from God nothing but love and favor, for Christ has pledged and given us his righteousness and everything he has; he has poured out upon us all his treasures, which no man can measure and no angel can understand or fathom, for God is a glowing furnace of love, reaching even from the earth to the heavens.

MARTIN LUTHER

This story is about a rag doll named Agnes, who ran into a grace-provider named Tony Campolo. Traveling in Hawaii but still on Eastern Standard Time, Tony wandered into a diner at three in the morning. The only other customers were a group of prostitutes who had finished for the night, one of whom (Agnes) mentioned that tomorrow was her birthday, and that she had never in her life had a birthday party.

After they left, Tony found out from Harry, the guy behind the counter, that they came each night to this diner. Tony asked if he could come back the next night and throw a party. Harry said okay, but only on the condition that his wife do the cooking and he be allowed to make the cake. What follows is a slightly abridged version of the story.

At 2:30 the next morning, I was back at the diner. I had picked up some crepe-paper decorations at the store and had made a sign out of big pieces of cardboard that read, "Happy Birthday, Agnes!"

The woman who did the cooking must have gotten the word out on the street, because by 3:15 every prostitute in Honolulu was in the place. It was wall-to-wall prostitutes . . . and me!

At 3:30 the door of the diner swung open and in came Agnes and her friend. I had everybody ready, and when they came in we all screamed "Happy Birthday!"

Never have I seen a person so flabbergasted. Her mouth fell open, and her legs buckled. When we finished singing, her eyes moistened; when the cake was carried out, she started to cry.

Harry gruffly mumbled, "Blow out the candles, Agnes. Come on! If you don't blow out the candles, I'm gonna hafta blow out the candles." Finally, he did. The cutting of the cake took even longer. "Cut the cake, Agnes. We all want some cake."

"Look, Harry, is it OK if I keep the cake a little while; if we don't eat it right away?"

"Sure. If you want to keep it, keep it. Take the cake home if you want."

"Can I?" Then, looking at me: "I just live down the street. I want to take the cake home, OK? I'll be right back."

She carried that cake out the door like it was the Holy Grail. We stood there motionless, a stunned silence in the place. Not knowing what else to do, I broke the silence by saying, "What do you say we pray?"

Looking back on it now, it seems more than strange for a sociologist to be leading a prayer meeting with a bunch of prostitutes in a diner in Honolulu at 3:30 in the morning. But then it just felt like the right thing to do. I prayed for Agnes; for her salvation, that her life would be changed. That God would be good to her.

When I finished, Harry leaned over the counter and said with a trace of irritation: "Hey, you never told me you were a preacher. What kind of church do you belong to?"

In one of those moments when just the right words come, I answered, "I belong to a church that throws birthday parties for prostitutes at 3:30 in the morning."

Harry waited a moment, and almost sneered as he answered, "No you don't. There's no church like that. If there was, I'd join it."

Wouldn't we all? Wouldn't we all love to join a church that throws birthday parties for prostitutes at 3:30 in the morning?

That's the kind of church Jesus came to create. I don't know where we got the other one that's so prim and proper. But anyone who reads the New Testament knows Jesus loved to lavish grace on the left-out and the used-up and the put-down. The sinners loved him because he partied with them. The lepers of society found in him someone they could eat and drink with.

This is the church the way it's supposed to be. A group of rag dolls who have received love even though they know they didn't deserve it, who then extend it to others because they refuse to allow raggedness to keep them from loving. Because love is God's signature. And grace makes love strong.

Philip Yancey relates a question posed by Gordon MacDonald during a conversation with him: What is the one thing the church has to offer that the world cannot get anywhere else?

After all, MacDonald notes, you don't have to be a Christian to build homes for the homeless, feed the poor, or donate to charity. You don't have to be a Christian to try to effect political change or pass social legislation. There are other traditions and teachers that offer wise moral instruction.

What's the one thing that the church has to offer that the world cannot get anywhere else?

Grace.

Where else can the world go to find grace?

We do not live in a grace-filled world. In this world, you get what you pay for. You reap what you sow. No free lunch. Eye for an eye. Quid pro quo.

> Living in grace, remembering grace, keeps love alive.

When is the last time you drove on a busy expressway and saw grace? How often do people roll the windows down and say, "Grace to you. I forgive you for cutting me off. I turn the other bumper. You ask for my lane, I'll give you the shoulder as well"? When is the last time an umpire blew a close call against the home team and a stadium full of people said, "Now is no time to be judgmental. Now more than ever we need to extend grace to this official. *Forgive the umpire!*" Not likely. The level of ungrace is so high that even to say "Maim the umpire" would be a step in the direction of mercy.

Living in grace, remembering grace, keeps love alive. But losing touch with grace, forgetting that I am loved because God is a gracious God, is a love-killer.

Sheldon Van Auken wrote, "The best argument for Christianity is Christians: their joy, their certainty, their completeness." Guess what he said is the best argument against it?

"When Christians are sombre, joyless, self-righteous, smug, narrow, repressive — Christianity dies a thousand deaths."

I think the following, by Dallas Willard, are some of the wisest words about the danger of grace-less spiritual life written in our time:

> How many people are radically and permanently repelled from the way by Christians who are unfeeling, stiff, unapproachable, boring, lifeless, obsessive, and dissatisfied? Yet such Christians are everywhere; and what they are missing is

the wholesome liveliness springing up from a balanced vitality within God's loving rule. **Spirituality wrongly understood or pursued is a major source of human misery and rebellion against God.**

Spirituality rightly understood is life. It is the humble reception of grace and the confident embrace of love.

Spirituality wrongly understood is death: a major source of human misery and rebellion against God. Spirituality wrongly understood leads to the most dangerous kind of raggedness. Spirituality wrongly understood produces people who mistake their lack of love for righteous superiority. It produces people who think their rags are actually righteousness. Let's consider some "spiritual" rag dolls, people whose deep raggedness is hidden under a veneer of spirituality wrongly understood.

"SPIRITUAL" RAG DOLLS

He was an angry man — angry toward his children, the people he worked with, the people he had gone to church with his whole life. He got into fights over points of doctrine, over what the sign in front of the church should say, over what the church motto should be.

His main reason to listen to sermons was not to encounter God or be broken by God, but to see where he might be able to point out flaws in them.

People outside the church wouldn't tolerate him because he was obnoxious. Inside the church, though, his obnoxiousness was regarded as zeal for truth.

He was regarded as a spiritual giant, but he could not love.

She was the most feared person in the church. She was a master at guilt and manipulation. She led a Bible study for women, but it was clear they were welcome only if they'd do what she would say. She was involved in a lot of people's lives but didn't love them. The truth is, she didn't even *like* them.

Everybody knew that at home she called all the shots, though ironically she was very devoted to a system that said the husband was ruler of the roost. In her home, therefore, her husband was boss — because she *said* he was, and heaven help him when he didn't boss the way she wanted him to. She submitted him right into the ground.

She was regarded as a spiritual giant, but she could not love.

He is a Christian leader and author who views himself as a defender of truth. He delights in ripping apart other Christians who disagree with any of his doctrinal positions. He doesn't just oppose their opinions, he caricatures their positions, twists their statements, maligns their motives. He wants to believe bad things about them. He also wants to believe bad things about political figures he disagrees with. He repeats such rumors and spreads them even if he's not sure they're true. He slanders truth in the name of defending truth.

He is regarded as a spiritual giant, but he cannot love.

She lived to complain. She complained about her grown children, who did not treat her right, about her neighbors, money, change, and life in general.

When her church went through changes she would oppose them, not so much because she didn't like the change as because changes might mean she was less in control. The changes were opening the church up to unchurchy people she didn't want there, people who didn't look or think or dress or vote like she did.

> Every one of us has our own raggedness.

Not too long ago at that church there was a church split. It involved ugly and vicious behavior, and the body of Christ was cut in two. The changes that had threatened her sense of control were gone, along with all the unchurched people. Things were as churchy and stilted and inaccessible to those on the outside as ever before.

And this was her comment to a friend: "Isn't it wonderful? We got our church back!"

She is regarded as a spiritual giant, but she cannot love.

What's most troubling is not that such people exist. Every one of us has our own raggedness. God knows I have edges more ragged than these.

What's most troubling is not that such people exist in the church. The church is a place for ragged people.

What's most troubling is that in church after church these people are not thought of as weaker brothers and sisters who need remedial help. They would be grossly offended to be thought or spoken of that way.

What's troubling is that they were looked up to as examples of what it means to be spiritual. They were what other people thought they were supposed to become. People were intimidated by them as paradigms of spiritual superiority. People got discouraged and thought perhaps they didn't really want to be spiritual because they did not want to end up looking like such as these. People were wounded or defeated or placed in despair by the raggedness of Christianity without grace.

Spirituality rightly understood? This is a life of wonder, awe, joy, simplicity, worship, gratitude, servanthood, humility, courage, and truth. Always its central characteristic is love.

> "Love the Lord your God with all your heart, and with all your soul, and with all your strength, and with all your mind, and your neighbor as yourself."
>
> "And if I have prophetic powers, and understand all mysteries and all knowledge, and if I have all faith, so as to remove mountains, but do not have love, I am nothing."
>
> "Whoever does not love does not know God, for God is love."

When Jesus explained spirituality rightly understood, people left everything: they gave up their possessions, sacrificed their careers, renounced past behavior and sin, accepted persecution and suffering, and they did it with joy. They did it laughing and weeping and high-fiving and dancing, because they had been loved in spite of themselves. They did it because they were convinced that here at last was the pearl of great price, this was the winning lottery ticket, this at long last was *it*. Jesus was *it*.

Spirituality wrongly understood produces people who are smug, self-righteous, unable to love, unable to feel. It produces cold hearts, plastic masks, sad faces, inauthentic lives, and shriveled souls.

Not long ago in my marriage, one of the two of us wanted for us to take dancing lessons. The other one of us said yes, because that one is a gracious person, and because it was a way of earning bonus points; kind of like matrimonial frequent-flyer miles that can be cashed in later.

Our instructor was a classically trained dancer from Eastern Europe. She was not capable of an awkward step or gesture. Her every move was poetry.

> The world is tired of Christians who proclaim that they know the right beliefs and are committed to the right values but in whom there is no grace.

I paid attention to every word she said. I tried to obey every command she gave. I counted the beat like a human metronome. I knew what I was supposed to do. And I tried doing it.

But I was counting out loud and staring at my feet, and my tongue was hanging out like Michael Jordan on his way to the hoop. I felt stiff and clumsy. I knew my raggedness.

The instructor told me something was lacking. In a single word, that something was grace. (What she actually said was along the lines of "balance, coordination, and the ability to make gross-motor movements without imperiling the well-being of others in the room," but it amounts to the same thing.)

The world is tired of Christians who proclaim that they know the right beliefs and are committed to the right values but in whom there is no grace.

Without grace, life is a clumsy, awkward business.

Without grace, people get hurt.

Victor Hugo's *Les Miserables* is the story of the triumph of God's gracious love over human raggedness. The escaped convict Jean Valjean, imprisoned for twenty years because he stole a loaf of bread, is shown hospitality by a bishop. But the temptation is too much; he takes some of the bishop's silver and steals away into the night. Stopped by a constable he tries to lie his way out of trouble: The silver was a gift, he says. The constable takes him back to the bishop and Jean Valjean waits to hear the words that will return him to prison until he dies. Nothing in his life prepared him for what he is about to hear.

"You are mistaken," the bishop says to Valjean. "Of course this silver was my gift. But only part. You forgot the most valuable part. You forgot to take the silver candlesticks."

Jean Valjean waits for the condemnation that he knows he deserves. Instead he is blindsided by grace. One moment he faces poverty and prison, the next freedom and abundance. Before Valjean leaves, the bishop says to him, "You must never forget this moment. Your soul and your life have been bought back. You are not your own. From now on, you belong to God."

And because of grace, Jean Valjean's life becomes an act of love. He honors the promise given to a dying prostitute: he devotes himself to raising her child, Cosette. Later he faces peril to save the man who loves Cosette, even though he knows it may mean living life alone.

Opposed to Jean Valjean is a man committed to the law, to "spirituality wrongly understood"; the constable Jauvert. Jauvert is convinced of his own righteousness. An eye for an eye, a tooth for a tooth. He is a champion of morality and justice. He spends his life seeking to recapture Jean Valjean.

Let us give Jauvert his day in court. He believes in many good things. He is committed to truth. He wants wrongdoing stamped out. He desires a society without thievery or deceit or corruption. He makes personal sacrifices to pursue such a society. He sincerely believes himself to be an agent of good.

In his world, though, there is no room for grace. And because he is blind to his own need for grace, his capacity to love withers and dies. He cannot offer mercy. The crisis of his existence occurs when Jean Valjean risks his own life to save that of Jauvert, his relentless pursuer. But Jauvert cannot bring himself to receive grace. He despairs. He kills himself, rather than admit the truth: his own raggedness has been as great as that of the criminals he devoted his life to punishing.

In the end it is Valjean, the convict, who is able to love. He comes to see what is expressed so beautifully in the musical *Les Miz*: "To love another person is to see the face of God."

Grace is the one thing the church has to offer that cannot be obtained anywhere else. This is why the New Testament is so full of it.

It came one day to a rag doll named Paul. He had the most dangerous kind of raggedness, one peculiar to religious people: He didn't know he was ragged. He thought God loved him because he merited being loved: "circumcised on the eighth day, a member of the people of Israel, of the tribe of Benjamin, a Hebrew born of Hebrews; as to the law, a Pharisee; as to zeal, a persecutor of the church; as to righteousness under the law, blameless." It was apparent to Paul that God was getting a pretty good deal in him. Like Jauvert, he devoted his life to pursuing and punishing those who were not devoted to the law as he was.

He was sure of what he believed, he was passionately committed to his values.

But something was missing.

Until Paul met grace. Or rather, grace met him. Then Paul realized that all these achievements — not bad on their own — had created pride and judgment in his heart. They had moved him away from love for God and love for people. Then he realized that his best righteousness was as filthy rags.

Then he had to do a radical audit. He said all these former assets he now considered *skubala*, a hard word to translate. "Rubbish" and "dung" and even "excrement" are used, but they're a little too polite; they don't capture the scorn Paul feels. It's really a bumper sticker word: *Skubala* happens. Anything that would keep Paul from living in grace — no matter how good it otherwise might be — is *skubala*.

REMEMBERING I'M LOVED BY GRACE

Paul is called the apostle of grace because he couldn't stop writing about it. In the space of a few verses in his letter to Colossae he uses a series of metaphors to convey the wonder of God's gracious love.

> God desires you for his family. Today. This is the wonder of grace.

He understood one of the most important things that I as a Christian must do is to remember not only that was I saved by grace, but that I am loved *this day* by grace. God did not save me by grace only to decide that now he will base how he feels about me on my spiritual performance yesterday. God's love is *always* a gracious love.

He speaks of circumcision and baptism, the initiation rites by which we have been included in a new community.

We have all known the pain of being on the outside, of not being wanted when they chose up teams, of being spurned by someone we love or forgotten by someone we thought was a friend, of being held at arm's length by someone in your family, maybe even your spouse.

Now God himself says you are chosen. You are wanted. God desires you for his family. Today. This is the wonder of grace.

By grace, Paul says, we have been made alive. You were dead to God: you had awe but no one to worship; guilt but no one to forgive you; desire for purpose but no one to serve; fear but no source of hope.

Now you are alive to God. You have strength to endure, power to serve, a reason to hope. Death itself has no hold over you. This is the wonder of grace.

By grace, Paul says, we are forgiven; the "certificate of indebtedness" has been nailed to the cross, utterly erased. Ever seen a check (not one of yours, of course) marked "insufficient funds"? (My mother says that in the early days of her marriage, when she got a statement that their checking account was overdrawn, she sent the bank a check for the difference.)

This is grace for anyone who's ever despaired over sin. This is the removal of our mountain of moral indebtedness. If you've ever felt that gap between reality and who you're called to be, ever felt like you can't close it — this is grace for you. God took our indebtedness and guilt and nailed it to the cross. He erased the bill, destroyed the IOU, so you are free. Unburdened. Cleansed. You can live with a heart as light as a feather. Today — no matter what you did yesterday. This is the wonder of grace.

By grace, Paul says, the "rulers and authorities" that threaten human flourishing have been "disarmed" and made a "public example" by Christ's crucifixion and resurrection. This is a military metaphor.

When a Roman general triumphed, he would parade through the streets of Rome. He would disarm the defeated generals, and they would have to march at the end of the parade. (They were not happy about this, of course.) They were tributes — willing or not — to the victory of the conqueror.

At the crucifixion and resurrection of Christ, Paul says, something happened. Powers that arranged themselves against human beings since the Fall — Paul is gloriously vague here so we can include them all — death, guilt, evil, spiritual powers, financial powers, political powers, systems and structures — have been disarmed of power to cause ultimate harm. "Who will separate us from the love of Christ?" Paul asks and concludes that nothing on the list has the power to do it.

Jesus' resurrection was the beginning of a parade. The end of it hasn't gotten to our block yet, but it's coming.

Therefore, Paul says, we can live in joy. We can have unshakable confidence — today, tomorrow, the next day, and every day through eternity. We can offer love to every human being, however ragged. This is the wonder of grace.

For Paul, the church is simply the custodian of grace.

"Grace" is how he started all his letters. Normally Greek letters started with the word *chairein* — "Greetings." It was a throwaway, a cliché, much as we start letters by saying, "Dear . . . ," whether the addressee is dear to us or not.

Paul changed this custom by starting with a new word for "grace," similar in form, *charis,* but radically different in meaning. "May grace be sent to you."

And he would end with the same word: "May the grace of our Lord Jesus Christ be with your spirit"; "may grace linger in your midst."

Grace is his invocation; grace is his benediction, grace is everything in between.

Grace is what knocked Paul to the ground on the road to Damascus.

Grace is what brought him to his knees over his sin, and grace is what took his sin away.

Grace was the light that blinded him, and grace was the power that took the scales from his eyes.

Grace gave Paul a thorn in the flesh to keep him from being destroyed by his own arrogance, and grace made Paul's weakness the very home of God's strength.

"My grace is sufficient for you," God said, and for Paul grace is the first word and the last word and all the words in between. Paul never recovered from the wonder of grace.

All this brings us to a sobering question: If grace is the one thing the church has to offer, if there is no wonder like the wonder of grace, why do we leave it so easily? Why is it that churches filled with people who say they have been saved by grace can become such ungracious people? Why do we seem to produce more Inspector Jauverts than Jean Valjeans? Why is it if you ask someone outside the church what they associate with the word "Christian" (especially "evangelical"), they might mention a conservative political agenda or judgmentalism or self-righteousness but not grace-filled love?

I think it has at least partly to do with pride. This is a major theme in Scripture. The writers of Scripture tell us that "God opposes the proud, but gives grace to the humble." This is because only the humble want to receive it.

When we're desperate, when we know the extent of our need, we are open to grace. Tax collectors and prodigal sons fall to their knees easily.

Once we start to think of ourselves as having accomplished something, we want some credit for it. Once people are inside the club, they'd like to see the entrance requirements go up, or what's the point?

Not too long ago, there was a CEO of a Fortune 500 company who pulled into a service station to get gas. He went inside to pay, and when he came out he noticed his wife engaged in a deep discussion with the service station attendant. It turned out that she knew him. In fact back in high school before she met her eventual husband, she used to date this man.

The CEO got in the car, and the two drove in silence. He was feeling pretty good about himself when he finally spoke: "I bet I know what you were thinking. I bet you were thinking you're

glad you married me, a Fortune 500 CEO, and not him, a service
station attendant."

"No, I was thinking if I'd married him, *he'd* be a Fortune 500
CEO and *you'd* be a service station attendant."

He didn't want to think part of his accomplishments might
have happened because of her. He wanted credit. He wanted the
pride that goes with being a self-made man.

We want grace the old-fashioned way. We want to earn it.

WARNING: GRACE ABUSE

Another form of "spirituality wrongly understood" is what
might be called "grace abuse." This tendency is as old as the
church: How do you live in grace without abusing it? There is an
ancient tendency to make grace a license for sin.

One biblical writer put it like this: "Certain intruders have
stolen in among you, people . . . who pervert the grace of our
God into licentiousness and deny our only
Master and Lord, Jesus Christ." Part of that
tendency to pervert grace is our own sin-
fulness, part of it is misunderstanding what
grace is and what it is not. Jesus illustrated
grace in his story of the prodigal son.

> There is an
> ancient tendency
> to make grace a
> license for sin.

When the son was far from home,
he was distracted from his distance from
the father by money and friends and what Jesus called "dissolute
living."

One day he woke up and his money was gone, his so-called
friends had deserted him, a famine had hit the land. Soon he was
living in squalor and eating the slop he fed to pigs. That chain of
events drove him to his knees, brought him to his senses.

Do you recognize that chain of events for what it was? Yes,
it was grace.

"'Twas grace that taught my heart to fear, and grace my fears relieved," the old song "Amazing Grace" says. We don't often think of grace as something that instills fear, but the song is right.

Imagine someone who lies brazenly, cheats without scruple, lusts without regret, betrays friends to get ahead — and does it all in a spirit of defiance and mockery. Then one day he looks in a mirror and gets the first glimpse of the horror he's become. He trembles at his capacity for what is foul and twisted.

That trembling, that pain is the beginning of salvation. "'Twas grace that taught my heart to fear." *Then* "grace my fears relieved."

Note how Jesus did *not* tell the story. The story doesn't say that the father tracked his son down while he was still far off. It doesn't say that while the son still spent money in dissolute living, the father said, "Please take this robe, put this ring with the other jewelry, have the fatted calf at one of your parties."

> If you don't want to come home to the Father, you don't want grace.

No. First things first. The son must want to come home, not because he had to *earn* his father's grace, but because *grace always and only consists of that which will help someone come home to and be immersed in the love of the Father.*

So if you don't want to come home to the Father, you don't want grace.

When the son was partying, what he needed more than anything else — if he was to come home — was pain. So *pain* was a gift of grace. Then when the son was in pain, what he needed most was to be welcomed home. So the *party* was a gift of grace.

For grace always and only consists of what will help someone come home to the Father.

There is another way Jesus does *not* tell the story. The great preacher Fred Craddock once told the story of the prodigal son as it would be told without grace.

This time, the father goes to the elder brother, not the prodigal, and says, "For all your hard work, for your years of labor in the field, I will kill the fatted calf. You wear the robe, you try on the ring — receive what you have earned."

And a woman in back of church stood up and said, "That's the way the story should have been told."

But Jesus didn't tell it that way. The elder brother spews his resentment; the father opens his heart. We wait for the ending of the story — what will the elder brother do? Join the party or become the new runaway?

Jesus never says. He deliberately leaves the story unfinished. He is, of course, surrounded by elder brothers, and they will have to finish the story themselves. Elder brothers need as much grace as prodigal sons.

Grace always and only consists of what will help someone come home to the Father.

This is why Dietrich Bonhoeffer wrote that there is no tension between discipleship and grace, correctly understood. Grace, he said, is simply the free offer of discipleship. Discipleship is simply the appropriation of grace. You can't have one without the other. But this is often misunderstood.

A man contemplated having an affair. He said to me, "I'm going to do this. It may be wrong, but God has to give me grace."

Grace is just what that man *doesn't* want. He doesn't want to come to his senses and repent. What he wants is pain-avoidance.

Grace is not pain-avoidance, but many people have accepted this warped view of grace. They go on year after year in chronic disobedience; letting anger fly without regard for consequences; allowing sinful relational patterns to go unchecked; refusing to live as a steward of time and money, blatantly using it the way they want to, disregarding the Spirit's leading, all in the name of "grace."

We live this way under the misguided notion that grace means having God over a barrel, cleverly taking advantage of the gospel. This attitude brings a tragic misunderstanding of God, sin, the gospel — and grace.

If you've been embracing this false notion of grace, it's time to stop. Now. Resolve to do what needs to be done to be at home with the Father.

LIVING IN GRACE

Finally, how can you and I remember that the love that sustains us is love based on grace?

We need to stay close to the cross. We need to regularly and honestly examine ourselves, confess our sins and shortcomings, and accept God's word of forgiveness.

Wise writers on the spiritual life often used to counsel people on the need to reflect on the cross, on the death of Christ. It is much harder to be ungracious to people, to refuse to forgive others, when we're standing in the shadow of the cross.

We also need to stay close to those who might be called "grace-providing" people. We need some people who accept us, welcome us, and love us, no matter what. I need some grace-providers. You do too.

> It is much harder to be ungracious to people, to refuse to forgive others, when we're standing in the shadow of the cross.

You need them because you have other kinds of people in your life. You have some "grace-impaired" people in your life, who will judge you and critique you and remind you of your raggedness in ways that will tear you down.

I was with a group of acquaintances some time ago and spoke of being lonely. I talked about this with some emotion, for I felt it quite deeply, but it was only a brief discussion.

Later, one member of this group asked me to go to lunch. "I wanted to talk to you about your loneliness," he told me. "I felt so sad when you said that." And there were tears in his eyes.

Suddenly it seemed as if someone else were bearing a burden that I had felt so heavily. I was so moved by his heart that *I* had tears. I was crying, he was crying — our server came over to see if perhaps something was wrong with the food.

He has become for me a dispenser of grace: someone who rejoices when I rejoice and mourns when I mourn.

How do you recognize these grace-providers? Grace-providers *notice* things about you; they pay attention to your heart and life. Grace-providers speak truthfully to you — both easy words and hard ones. Grace-providers are not people who only say what you want to hear, but they speak the truth in love.

Grace-providers simply never cease to love you. They see beneath the surface; they see the darkness as well as the goodness in your heart. But when they see the darkness they do not pull away. They are not repulsed. They move toward you. You may be a rag doll, but you are God's rag doll, and grace-providers never let you forget it.

Especially, I need to stay close to the ultimate Grace-provider. John says that when Jesus became human "the Word became flesh and lived among us, and we have seen his glory, the glory as of a father's only son, full of grace and truth."

He was full of truth. He knew the right thing. He did the right thing. Finally the human race saw somebody who knew the right thing, did the right thing, and whose knowing and doing were filled with grace.

People who had devoted their lives to spirituality wrongly understood were offended by him. His comment about them was, "We played the flute for you, and you did not dance." But every once in a while, somebody got it. And the dance would go on.

You see, it was grace that was wrapped in swaddling clothes and laid in a manger. It was grace that dwelt among us, grace that healed the sick, cured the blind, and raised the dead. It was grace that partied with ragged tax collectors, grace that was called friend of sinners, grace that would not cast the first stone. It was grace that was nailed to the cross along with our sin and guilt, grace that the tomb could not hold, grace that now sits on the right hand of the Father, grace that will one day come back for you and me.

When we've been there 10,000 years and every other word has been used up and worn out, we will just be starting to sing about grace.

NINE

BEING LOVED MEANS
BEING CHOSEN

The one who loves flies, runs, and is glad; he is free and not bound. He gives all for all, and has all in all, because he rests in one who is supreme above all things, from whom every good thing flows and goes forth.

THOMAS À KEMPIS

To be loved means to be chosen. The sense of being chosen is one of the very best gifts love bestows on the beloved. It means someone has seen me as a unique person, and that someone desires to come closer to me, to be on the same side as I'm on. Someone believes I have a significant contribution to make.

On the other hand, there is no pain quite like the pain of not being chosen. The day I'm writing this a ten-year-old has written to Dear Abby about the pain of life on the playground: "All my life I have been chosen last. That's my problem. . . . Why don't they just hang a sign on me that says, 'Reject. Last one to pick gets me.'"

There is no gift like being chosen, no pain like rejection. And when a reject is chosen by someone, a life gets changed. The following is from a book called *The Whisper Test*:

> I grew up knowing I was different, and I hated it. I was born with a cleft palate, and when I started school, my classmates made it clear to me how I looked to others: a little girl with a misshapen lip, crooked nose, lopsided teeth, and garbled speech.

When schoolmates asked, "What happened to your lip?" I'd tell them I'd fallen and cut it on a piece of glass. Somehow it seemed more acceptable to have suffered an accident than to have been born different. I was convinced that no one outside my family could love me.

There was, however, a teacher in the second grade whom we all adored — Mrs. Leonard by name. She was short, round, happy — a sparkling lady.

Annually we had a hearing test . . . Mrs. Leonard gave the test to everyone in the class, and finally it was my turn. I knew from past years that as we stood against the door and covered one ear, the teacher sitting at her desk would whisper something, and we would have to repeat it back — things like "The sky is blue" or "Do you have new shoes?" I waited there for those words that God must have put into her mouth, those seven words that changed my life. Mrs. Leonard said, in her whisper, "I wish you were my little girl."

Love confers a kind of chosenness on the one who is loved. Love whispers, *I choose you. I want to be on your side.* And for ragged people, for people with misshapen spirits and crooked hearts and lopsided souls, this is life.

Being chosen involves four factors, three of them positive.

When I am chosen, I am seen as unique. Objects may be indistinguishable from each other; one brick is pretty much like another, and bricks are eminently replaceable. But each human being cries out to be noticed as special, as not just one more of the same.

When I am chosen, I am recognized as someone who has something to contribute. My uniqueness is positive. I have a gift that will make a difference. I have something that will help the team. Chosen people are significant. Their biographies get written and read because their stories matter.

When I am chosen, it means somebody wants *me.* I am not isolated, unconnected. I am desired. I belong.

When God chooses us he imparts all the good implied by the choosing. In our fallen world, however, the term *chosen* has a fourth implication that is not present in the heart of God. To be chosen in our world almost always means to be chosen at the expense of someone else. To be chosen in our world means to be better than or superior to, to be the object of jealousy, to be the favorite. In our world, the scramble for chosenness becomes a competitive game. And the consolation prize for the losers is a malignant little creature known as envy. Homecoming queens and first-round draft choices, these are the chosen ones. Rag dolls need not apply.

Our life is a constant struggle: Will I be chosen or rejected? How quickly will I be selected when we choose up sides for baseball? Will she say yes when I ask her out? Will I be selected for this school, that job, this promotion?

In this world, the value of "chosenness" goes up in proportion to how many others are rejected for the same status. If one woman is chosen "Miss America" it means fifty others are rejected, not to mention all the thousands who never made it to the final pageant. Chosenness comes at the expense of others' rejection. I remember when I finished graduate school, those who had not yet passed the final exams to become licensed psychologists always hoped the bar was set quite low. Once people passed, this wish had a way of being reversed. Now they wanted the bar set as high as possible to keep the riffraff out. Once I'm in the club, I want to keep it as exclusive as possible — or what's the point of being in? This is why Groucho Marx once said he would never join a club whose standards were so low they would accept him as a member.

WHAT GAME WILL I PLAY?

Robert Roberts writes about a fourth grade class where the teacher introduced a game called the "balloon stomp." A balloon was tied to every child's leg, and the object of the game was to pop everybody else's balloon while protecting your own. The last person with an intact balloon wins.

Balloon stomp is a zero-sum game. If I win, you lose. Anyone else's successes diminish my chances. I must regard everyone else as someone to overcome, someone to be rooted against.

Balloon stomp is a Darwinian contest — the survival of the fittest — and since ten-year-olds are Darwinian people, they entered into the spirit of the thing vigorously. Balloons were relentlessly targeted and destroyed. A few of the children hung shyly on the sidelines, but their balloons were doomed just the same. The battle was over in a matter of seconds. Only one balloon was still inflated, and of course, its owner was the most disliked kid in the room. It's hard to really win at balloon stomp.

Then, Roberts writes, a disturbing thing happened. A second class was brought in the room to play the same game, only this time it was a class of mentally handicapped children. They too were each given a balloon, they were given the same instructions, the same signal began the game. "I got a sinking feeling in my midsection," said one of the onlookers. "I wanted to spare the kids the pressure of a competitive brawl."

This time, though, the game proceeded differently. The instructions were given too quickly to be grasped very well by these children. In all the confusion the one idea that sank in was that the balloons were supposed to be popped. But instead of fighting each other off, these children got the idea that they were supposed to help one another pop balloons. So they formed a kind of balloon stomp co-op. One little girl knelt down and held her balloon carefully in place, like the holder for a field-goal kicker, while a little boy stomped it flat. Then he knelt down and held his balloon still for her to stomp. On and on it went, all the children helping one another in the Great Stomp.

And when the very last balloon was popped, everybody cheered.

Everybody won.

The question you have to ask is, who got the game right, and who got the game wrong?

The question you have to answer is, which game are you going to play?

In God's plan, your chosenness enriches me instead of diminishing me. Israel was called God's chosen people, but not in the sense that they were his favorites or that they had an inside track to heaven. His plan as expressed at the very beginning was that through Abraham "all the people of the earth should be blessed." Israel was chosen not *instead of* the other nations of the earth but precisely *for the sake of* the other nations of the earth. God's plan was that as his community is incarnated on earth, all the peoples on earth should be drawn to it.

This was the realization that rocked Peter when it finally dawned on him, "I now realize how true it is that God does not show favoritism but accepts men from every nation who fear him and do what is right."

But our world plays a different game. Historian Christopher Lasch wrote that we are living in "the culture of *competitive individualism*, which in its decadence has carried the logic of individualism to the extreme of *a war of all against all*, the pursuit of happiness to the dead end of a narcissistic preoccupation with the self."

Recently I've come to see how often I play this game. So many of my initial thoughts and knee-jerk reactions when I see people are judgmental, comparative, competitive, and lead me away from love.

I see someone driving an expensive car and I find myself thinking, *She probably has too much money; she's probably materialistic.* If anyone has a car much more expensive than mine, I'm likely to think automatically that it's a reflection of a materialistic lifestyle.

By contrast, when someone is driving a car that is older and worse than mine, I'm likely to think, *Here is someone who probably does not function on as high a level as I do. Probably this person is not as successful as I am.* (I think it was comedian George Carlin who noted that everyone driving faster than you is an idiot, while everyone driving slower is a moron.)

Someone is complaining, and I think, *He's probably needy, a victim type. I better stay clear. Why can't he be more mature?*

If I find someone who is always cheerful, I'm likely to think, *This guy is too happy. He's probably living in denial.*

I'll find myself thinking of someone else, *This person has something I want. I wish I had his brains* (or looks, or success, or marriage, or money).

Or I wish he didn't. If I can't have these things, I'd be happier if no one did.

Stomp!

These thoughts lead me to judge or to gossip or to be unloving. They lead me to play the wrong game.

A STUDY IN ENVY

Early in Jesus' ministry we are told that the disciples of John the Baptist came to John and said, "Rabbi, the one who was with you across the Jordan, to whom you testified, here he is baptizing, and all are going to him."

John's disciples were very concerned because John's ratings were down. For some time he had been the hottest thing on the circuit, but the latest Neilsen ratings confirmed he was in danger of losing his status as a prime-time player. He was no longer number one at the box office.

Sports psychologists speak of the practice of basking in "reflected" glory. Rabid fans have their own sense of self-esteem enhanced when the team wins. When their team loses, they become depressed. When the team becomes a chronic loser, fans will actually go to the games wearing a paper bag over their heads. No one wants to be identified with a loser.

John's disciples had most likely been basking in reflected glory. If John the Baptist's status were to go down, guess who else's status would go down with it?

They needed John to be a Big Dog. If you can't be a Big Dog yourself, the next best thing is to associate with one. When you're the big dog — or associated with the Big Dog — you have status. You are important. Everybody else's position is determined by how they stack up next to the Big Dog. They were concerned that if current trends continued, they'd have to start looking for paper bags.

> Being chosen by God is not about grasping; it is about learning to let go.

But status and prominence — the externals of his success — are precisely what John will have to let go of. Being chosen by God is not about grasping; it is about learning to let go.

LETTING GO

One of the hardest things in life is learning to let go. When you're a parent, you think the hard part is taking care of your kids. That's not the hard part. The hard part is letting go of them.

The first day of school comes. You know your children are going to get bullied, going to be tempted, going to fail sometimes and be hurt sometimes. There will be some kids they don't get along with who may wound them, stupid teachers who don't like them, and you can't do a thing. You have to let them go. The first time they get in a car all by themselves, you have to let them go.

A bumper sticker says, "Let go and let God." "Let go" does not mean being passive or inactive. It means trust.

There's an old story about a man who falls off a cliff. He's going to die, but he throws out a hand and miraculously catches a branch:

"Is anyone up there?"

"Yes."

"Who are you?"

"I am God, and I am going to save you."

"Wonderful. What should I do?"

"Let go of the branch."

(Pause.) "Is anybody else up there?"

Letting go is always an act of trust. That is the case with John and his disciples. He's been the Big Dog, and they've been important because they've been hanging out with him. Earlier the question was, did he have enough faith to hang on, to keep preaching repentance when religious leaders opposed him. Now the question was even harder than being able to hang on: Did he have enough faith to let go?

> Letting go is always an act of trust.

If there was one thing John was an expert at, it was letting go. From his earliest days he knew he had been chosen by God for a special task. This chosenness would cost him everything. In order to carry out his ministry, John had to let go of all the normal hopes and aspirations of first-century life.

- He had to give up normal home life; we're told that he "was in the wilderness until he appeared publicly to Israel." No condo, no cable, no homeowner's association. This wasn't Palm Springs; in John's day the desert was the desert.
- He would never have a normal job. When he filled out paperwork all he could list under occupation was "fanatic."
- He had given up all financial hopes. His line of work did not offer much in the way of health benefits or pension plans.
- He had to let go of ordinary relationships; he was a stranger to society. He lived the life of a hermit, and hermits are not big networkers. There are no Dale Carnegie courses for hermits.

- God asked him to relinquish all claims to comfort, and this he had been willing to do as well. He was seriously fashion-challenged. He wore clothes that wouldn't make the cut at garage sales or thrift shops. His cuisine was enough to send Oprah back to Slim-Fast; locusts and wild honey was not much of a diet even by first-century standards. No Chablis with dinner, either. He was on the wagon before there were wagons. He was a teetotaler who didn't even get tea.
- He lived without security. He challenged the religious powers of his day in the most open terms, and they hated him for it. He would sometimes address his congregation as a snake pit, and this is not going to get you promoted to District Superintendent.

Imagine the liturgy:

  Leader: "You are a brood of vipers."
  People: "We are a brood indeed."

He would eventually confront the governor over his immorality and corruption, and in those days you didn't do that sort of thing if you were at all attached to your head.

- He had to let go of any hopes for a normal home life. He would never fall in love, never be married, never have children. There would be no one to watch over him should he grow old. In fact he had to relinquish dreams of growing old, as well. John had been chosen by God from before his birth to prepare the way of the Lord. But it was a kind of chosenness that meant sacrifice and strangeness and confrontation and never fitting in. It was the kind of chosenness that caused Reb Tevye in *Fiddler on the Roof* to say to God, "I know, I know — we are your chosen people. But once in a while, couldn't you choose somebody else?"

All of this John was willing to let go of for the sake of his ministry. And now God was asking him to let go of one more thing: his ministry.

It seemed to his followers as if his very chosenness were now being lost.

John's followers came to him, apparently, because they were envious of Jesus' success. It was intolerable to them that after John had launched Jesus in the ministry, given Jesus John's own seal of credibility, Jesus should repay them by out-drawing John. They were so upset they could not speak without exaggeration: "Rabbi, the one who was with you across the Jordan, to whom you testified, here he is baptizing, and *all* are going to him."

It was bad enough that Jesus should start offering his own independent baptism ministry after John had had the exclusive franchise, but now *everyone* was going to Jesus.

THE ANATOMY OF ENVY

Envy is the toxic bile of those who feel themselves to be unchosen. Harold Boris writes, "Envy . . . carries with it a particular sort of misery: Not only do we feel deficient and defective and filled with hate but in our aloneness, by our aloneness, we feel diminished, even humiliated."

Envy is wanting what another person has and feeling badly that I don't have it. Envy is disliking God's goodness to someone else and dismissing God's goodness to me. Envy is desire plus resentment. Envy is anticommunity. Paul said that we are to "rejoice with those who rejoice; mourn with those who mourn." Envy causes me to mourn when others rejoice and rejoice when others mourn.

Envy is dangerous because it is opposed to other people. Sins like greed and lust are simply about the gratification of *my* desires. Envy not only seeks self-gratification, but it seeks to diminish the one I envy. Samuel Rogers was a nineteenth-century British poet who knew about envy. A gathering of society leaders was praising one of its members who was absent, a young duke who had looks, talent, wealth, and a promising future. In a brief pause Rogers said, "Thank God he has bad teeth!"

Stomp!

Envy by its nature can never be appeased. Indulging envy is like trying to quench your thirst by drinking salt water.

Of all emotions, envy may be the most humiliating, because it is so small-minded. Frederick Buechner says, "Envy is the consuming desire to have everybody else as unsuccessful as you are."

> Indulging envy is like trying to quench your thirst by drinking salt water.

When I envy someone, I lose sight of their humanity. When Cain looks at Abel, he no longer sees a brother. Abel is now only the rival who threatens Cain's status before God. Abel is the hated favorite. It is the balloon stomp game taken to the final extreme. Envy isolates — it's every man for himself.

Envy is the reversal of empathy. In empathy, I seek to put myself in the place of another person. Envy causes me to seek to absorb the other person. In empathy, I seek to sacrifice myself for the sake of the other. In envy, I seek to sacrifice the other for the sake of myself.

John must have wondered of his followers, *Do they really love me, or are they just using me?*

And of course, as in all human relationships, it was some of both.

Surely when they heard the message of this lonely, fiery prophet who called for hard repentance and severe renewal, something inside them was stirred, something felt called.

But they were human. They wanted John to be important so they could be important. And they ended up trying to move him from his true calling. They wanted him to make sure he was bigger than the Messiah.

For just as Jesus knew temptation in the desert, so did his friend John. This was John's trial. For Jesus, the temptation was to turn stones into bread, throw himself from the temple, bow down and worship Satan. Do something spectacular. Later on temptation would come from his friend Peter: Avoid the cross, bypass suffering, travel from strength to strength.

For John, the temptation took this form: Do something big to win the people back. Adjust your message; change your marketing strategy. The way to measure your success is by the number of people baptized, like McDonald's measures it in numbers of hamburgers sold. Trust what is visible.

There was another message in their temptation, a little more subtle, but present: Jesus is our opponent. His ministry is your rival. For him to be bigger means you will be smaller, and this is intolerable.

His followers loved John, perhaps, but it was a ragged sort of love. And it would have destroyed him if he'd listened to it.

THE SUBTLETY OF ENVY

Envy is pernicious because it can extend to everything. I can even envy another person's spirituality or humility.

Harold Boris writes of three men who came to pay their respects to the Lord. As befit his station in life, the one who was arrayed in gold was the first to present himself at the altar.

"Forgive me, O Lord," he prayed. "I am nothing."

The second man stepped forward, dressed in silver. "O Lord, forgive me. I am nothing."

The third man came to the altar, clothed in rags, disheveled, robe tattered and torn. "O Lord," he prayed, "forgive me, for I am nothing."

At this the first man nudged the second. "Look who's calling himself nothing."

Stomp!

Saul was the warrior-king of Israel, and we're told that he stood "head and shoulders" above everyone else. After a while, you get used to being head and shoulders above others. You don't like it when someone else pokes their head where only yours belongs.

But it happens. A young man named David, not even large enough to wear Saul's armor, wins the ancient heavyweight championship against Goliath. David is a greater Terminator even than Saul. And a new song tops the charts: "Saul has killed his thousands, and David his ten thousands."

Saul did not care for the lyrics. He no longer viewed David as a person, as a shepherd boy. David was now the Enemy.

" 'They have ascribed to David ten thousands, and to me they have ascribed thousands; what more can he have but the kingdom?' So Saul eyed David from that day on."

As Neal Plantinga noted, "eyeing" is precisely what Saul did. He cast the evil eye of envy, which filters out humanity and leaves only a threat.

Envy is primarily a sin of the eye. It makes my brother's piece of cake look bigger and better than mine. A child may have a hundred toys, but envy makes the one toy that a sibling asks to play with the most desirable of all. When it comes to envy, the eyes have it. This is why Dante says that in hell, the envious must go through eternity with their eyes sewn shut.

A green thread of envy runs through the whole Bible: from Cain and Abel to Isaac and Ishmael to Jacob and Esau to Joseph and his brothers to Miriam and Aaron grumbling against Moses. Rachel was chosen; Leah was a rag doll with "weak eyes." Ahab coveted Naboth's vineyard; Ananias and Sapphira coveted a reputation for generosity; Paul wrote to the church at Philippi that there were people who actually preached "out of rivalry and envy."

That's a sobering line for me. There is envy in me. It makes no sense when it comes to preaching. In preaching I'm called to tell people to repent, to take up the cross and die to self. How could I be envious because other preachers can call people to die to themselves better than I can call people to die to themselves? But this chastising thought does not by itself make envy go away.

Envy makes us pursue things we don't even truly want. In *Siblings Without Rivalry*, one mom tells of a summer day when she was ridding a large freezer in the garage of a two-year frost build-up.

> The kids were in bathing suits. . . . I playfully tossed a big slab of ice in the direction of one of the kids and said, "Here, have some ice." Immediately the other two chimed in, "I want some too."
>
> I grabbed two more big slabs and slid them towards the other two. Then the youngest yelled, "They have more."
>
> I said, "You want more? Here's more!" and threw a potful of ice at his feet. Then the other two yelled, "Now *he* has more." I threw two more pots of ice in their direction. The first one cried, "Now *they* have more."
>
> By this time, all three children were ankle deep in ice and still yelping for more. As fast as I could I flung huge chunks of ice at everyone's feet. Even though they were hopping up and down in pain from the cold, they continued to scream for more, in a frenzy that one would gain an advantage over the other.
>
> That was when I realized how futile it was to ever try to make things equal. The children could never get enough, and as a mother, I could never give enough.

Envy can only be healed when I come to live as one who has been chosen by God.

I do not like the envy in me. I would make it go away if I could. But I cannot stop envying simply by trying hard. Envy can only be healed when I come to live as one who has been chosen by God.

One of the most important words in the Bible to describe God's people is *chosen*. "As God's *chosen* ones, holy and beloved," Paul writes to the Colossians.

In this world, those who are chosen rule. Those who are not chosen serve.

God does not choose in that way, though. In God's love, my chosenness never comes at anyone else's expense. God chooses, or loves, each of his children with infinite uniqueness. His plan is for my chosenness to enhance the lives of others, not diminish them. In God's plan those who are chosen are always chosen to serve.

Harold Boris writes of the possibility that envy is rooted in the fear that I am not chosen, that I was not "intended to be." Faber notes that the love children crave is not to be loved "equally" with siblings, for somehow equal always feels like less. "To be loved *uniquely* — for one's special self — is to be loved as much as we need to be loved." This is what God does: he loves each of us uniquely.

John understood this truth, and his reflection on it captures perfectly his sense of both who he is and who he is not. "No one can receive anything except what has been given from heaven," John said. I must come to understand the particular joy that I am able to receive.

I am not the groom, John says, I am the friend of the groom. In ancient Jewish weddings, the friend of the groom was his *shoshbin*, something like our best man. The *shoshbin* was in charge of many of the details of the wedding arrangements. He would often invite the people. He would accompany the groom to the ceremony. Then he had one last responsibility. On the final night of the wedding, he would stand guard over the tent where the bride waited for her groom. It would be dark, but the *shoshbin* recognized the groom's voice when he heard it. So the *shoshbin* would stand aside, get out of the way. The groom would go into the tent and know the joy of claiming his bride. The friend of the groom had a different joy, the joy of serving the one he loved. If the friend should envy the groom, if he should try to claim for himself the joy that belonged to the groom alone, he would lose everything. The bride could never belong to him, and in trying to claim her he would betray his friend and lose the joy that belonged to the *shoshbin* as well.

John said, in essence, to his followers, "The joy that belongs to the friend of the groom is my joy. I sent out the invitations. I was the one who cried in the wilderness, 'Prepare the way of the Lord.'

"I served the groom. He is my friend. Now he has come. I've heard his voice; he's come to claim his bride. This is the reason everyone is flocking to him. She is *his* bride, not mine. The joy of the bridegroom belongs to him.

> Envy always carries with it a sense of being victimized: "You *owe* me," envy says. "I *deserve* this."

"Don't think this is painful for me. I too have joy. My joy is the joy of the friend of the groom. If I were to try to seize his joy, I would end up with no joy at all. Now my joy is complete. I will not lose that. I will not allow envy to destroy my joy."

In the play *Amadeus*, Antonio Salieri is the court musician whose soul is destroyed by envy. He longs to create music for the ages, for the glory of God, and (not incidentally) for his own fame. The pain of his own mediocrity is intensified by the genius of Mozart and doubled because Mozart is portrayed as an impossibly foppish, coarse, flippant boor. Salieri's envy drives him to resentment, hatred, betrayal, and deception as he attempts to pass one of Mozart's works off as his own.

Salieri, like all first-class enviers, believes that God has been unforgivably unfair to him. Since he wanted to be greater than Mozart, he believes God had a moral obligation to make him greater than Mozart. Envy always carries with it a sense of being victimized: "You *owe* me," envy says. "I *deserve* this."

So Salieri claims his title, "the prince of mediocrity," as an indictment against an unjust God. No one, not even the priest to whom he confesses, is able to justify God's apparent injustice.

But the truth is, Salieri had the possibility of a great joy. He did not possess Mozart's gift. But he was offered another. He could have been the one to recognize Mozart's genius, to proclaim it to the world, to open doors and provide opportunities for Mozart that could have enriched his life and his world. He could have been the friend of the groom. But this joy he refused. He wanted only to be the groom, and so he ended his life with no joy at all.

> Envy is humanity at its most ragged.

The name *Amadeus* means "beloved of God." The pain of Salieri was that he believed another was beloved in place of him. The tragedy of Salieri was that he too could have lived as the beloved, if he had received the gift held out for him.

The same cancer was at work in the life of another Salieri named Herod the Great. When Jesus — the true "King of the Jews" — was born, Herod could have been the one to sponsor him, to see that he was educated and cared for. But this joy Herod refused. His envy drove him to hatred, deception, betrayal, and murder. And so it went all his life. Herod the Great was so hated that at the end of his life he left orders for seventy of the most prominent citizens of Jerusalem to be executed after his death so that there might be mourning after his passing.

Matthew tells us envy was the reason the religious leaders had Jesus put to death. Envy tried to prevent his birth, envy dogged his life, envy caused his death. Envy is humanity at its most ragged.

God holds out a certain joy for each of his children. For example, we can all share in the joy of the singer. As the gifted one sings, she shares her gift, and we receive it, all of us grateful to our Creator for lavishing this gift and allowing the singer to share it with us.

There is, however, one certain way to lose the joy of the listener, and that is to envy the joy of the singer, to wish that you were up there instead of her, to compare your gift to hers and feel that sinking sensation that the greater another person's gifts or talents or beauty, the more you are diminished. Live a life of comparison or competition, and you end up with no joy at all.

God holds out joy for each of us. We are all made to do and see things in a unique way — God has designed you to know the joy of being a teacher or helper or encourager or designer — and when you find it and offer it up you will know joy. And God has made you to know the joy of receiving and celebrating the gifts of those around you. If you offer your gifts (let go of them) and humbly receive the gifts of others, your joy will be made complete.

If you don't, if you go through life wishing for joy that belongs to others, you will end up with no joy at all.

John's final comment was this: "He must become greater; I must become less."

This is no statement of resignation or martyrdom. This is joy of the friend of the groom who realizes the bride has now entered her destiny. This is John's participation in the kingdom of God where the humble become exalted.

There is a reason why Christmas is celebrated December 25. It is not a historical date, of course, but neither was it chosen at random. It was chosen because it is the time of year when days begin to grow longer. The coming of Christ means the coming of light into the world; darkness is being rolled back. And in the days before electricity, the lengthening of daylight was a great gift. It brought light and warmth to a wintry world.

Do you know when, in the church calendar year, John the Baptist's birth is celebrated? June 24. Not a historical date, but not chosen at random. That's when the days begin to get shorter and the light begins to lessen.

Every year the calendar proclaims again the words of John, though few are aware of it.

"He must increase, but I must decrease."

But in the magnification of Christ is the hope of the world, including John. For in Christ God is drawing all men to himself. God whispers on the cross: "I wish you belonged to me. I choose you."

TEN

SAFE IN GOD'S LOVE

With this magnificent God positioned among us, Jesus brings us the assurance that our universe is a perfectly safe place to be.

DALLAS WILLARD

Some time ago I took my three children into the empty auditorium of the church where I work. We sat in the very back row, taking in the silence, when one of my children said, "Daddy, preach to us."

This was a wonderful moment, and it does not happen often in my family. It is a rare thing that Nancy and I will be in bed at night, and she'll roll over and say, "Preach to me, honey." This was a choice opportunity, so I thought carefully about what to say, because I wanted to get it right.

I wanted to tell them they could live in the loving care of God, so I told them the story of a movie called *The Bear*. It is the saga of a tiny bear cub whose mother dies. The cub survives, but the viewer knows that his long-term chances are nil. Then the unexpected happens. The little cub gets more or less adopted by an enormous kodiak. This giant is always watching over the cub. He protects it from a mountain lion that has been stalking him. He teaches the cub how to be a bear. Everything the father bear does, the cub imitates: he waddles in a stream and stabs at fish like the daddy bear, he stands on two legs and scratches his back against a tree as he's seen his father do. You watch this and are filled with hope — the cub has a future. He's going to live.

One day they get separated. The little bear can't see his father anywhere. The mountain lion has never forgotten the cub and now finally sees his opportunity. He comes swiftly, silently, face-to-face with the cub; he is about to spring. The little bear does what he has seen his father do: He rears up on his hind legs, lifts his paws, and tries to growl fiercely, but the best he can manage is a frightened squeak. The mountain lion is not convinced. Both the cub and his attacker know he is about to die.

> The father could be trusted, even when he seemed to be absent.

The camera focuses on the mountain lion, whose face suddenly registers a look of fear. He stops snarling, turns, and slinks away.

The camera returns to the cub. He is as surprised as anyone watching. Could the growl have worked so well? But then the camera pans back, and we see what we did not know was there; we see what the little bear cannot. Behind that little bear is the great kodiak, standing on his hind legs, his massive body poised to save his son with a single swipe.

Big paws. Fierce growl.

Then we know. The little bear had nothing to worry about. The cub couldn't see him or hear him, but the father was there all the time. That forest was a perfectly safe place for the little cub to be. The father could be trusted, even when he seemed to be absent.

CHARIOTS OF FIRE

Could this be true for you and me as well? The writer of 2 Kings tells of a time when the king of Aram, an enemy of Israel — a fierce mountain lion — sent a great army to surround the city of Dothan and destroy the prophet Elisha.

"Alas, master! What shall we do?" worried Elisha's servant.

Elisha responded with this remarkable statement: "Don't be afraid. Those who are with us are more than those who are with them." Elisha's servant looked around, perhaps, trying to figure out where the "those who are with us" were hiding.

But Elisha went on to pray, "God, open his eyes so that he may see."

Slowly the camera pans back. "Then the Lord opened the servant's eyes, and he looked and saw the hills full of horses and chariots of fire all around Elisha."

God's heart is filled with tenderness and delight at the mere thought of you.

Big paws. Fierce growl.

Elisha proceeded to ask for the Arameans to be blinded, which they were, and when they stopped to ask for directions he was the one they consulted. In a divine comedy of errors he hand-delivered them to the king of Israel, who asked Elisha, "Shall I kill them, my father? Shall I kill them?"

"Would you kill men you have captured with your own bow and arrow?" said Elisha slyly, as if bows and arrows had anything to do with it. "Set food and water before them so that they may eat and drink and then go back to their master."

So the Arameans had a big party and went home, and "the bands from Aram stopped raiding Israel's territory." Everybody ended up safe at home.

Elisha understood what his servant did not. They were surrounded by a loving protection the servant little dreamed of. His moment of greatest fear was really his time of greatest safety.

You live in the hand of God, I told my kids. God's heart is filled with tenderness and delight at the mere thought of you. When you love somebody and you think about them, it makes you smile. That's how it is for God when he thinks about you.

You will take risks in life, and you will face problems. This is part of life and growth, and I would not spare you from it if I could. But I do want to spare you from one thing. Sometimes when you are afraid you may be tempted to think you're all alone. You may think no one sees or cares, that you are on your own.

When that happens, I want you to remember the bear. Remember that Someone is watching over you. You may not be able to see or hear him. But you are never out of his sight. You are never out of his care.

You are the beloved of God.

PERFECTLY SAFE

Dallas Willard writes that Jesus lived a life of utter trust because he understood his Father to be unfailingly competent and wholly devoted. Here is the striking result: "With this magnificent God positioned among us, Jesus brings the assurance that our universe is a perfectly safe place for us to be."

Really? Our universe? We talk much in our day about safe places, because our world seems so unsafe. Catastrophes and violence and disease blanket the earth.

And yet this is the discovery that gets made over and over in the Scriptures. Lions' dens and fiery furnaces, Pharaoh's prison and the floor of the Red Sea, a battered little boat in the midst of a violent storm — all these seemed to be most dangerous, but turned out to be the safest places of all.

It really is true — our universe is a perfectly safe place for us to be. Not because bad things won't happen in it, but because, as Paul put it, "Who will separate us from the love of Christ? Will hardship, or distress, or persecution, or famine, or nakedness, or peril, or sword." The worst weapons that this world can unleash are powerless before that love.

This is the discovery of the psalmist: "Yea, though I walk through the valley of the shadow of death, I will fear no evil: for thou art with me." Even the valley of the shadow of death is a safe place.

Our little growls and snarls may not be much on their own, but behind us stands One whose watch is unceasing. We may not be able to see him or hear him, but the Father is there all the time.

And nothing can separate us from his love. Not failure. Or cancer. Or bankruptcy. Or loneliness. Or death itself.

Stronger than all these enemies, he stands behind and all around us. One day we'll hear the roar, we'll see the hands that even now hold us. Till then we walk by faith. But still it is true: We never stand alone.

A mother wakes up during a thunderstorm. She hurries to her son's room after a particularly bright flash of lightning, knowing he will be terrified. To her surprise, he is standing at a window.

"I was looking outside," he says, "and you'll never guess what happened. God took my picture."

He was convinced God was at work and therefore that the universe was a perfectly safe place for him to be.

Matthew tells us that Jesus and his followers were in a boat once when "without warning, a furious storm came up on the lake"; a not uncommon occurrence on the Sea of Galilee. The disciples were understandably frantic, but the text says Jesus was taking a nap.

Why does Matthew include the information that Jesus was sleeping? Because Matthew wants us to understand. Given what he knew about the Father, Jesus was convinced that the universe was a perfectly safe place for him to be.

The disciples had faith in Jesus. They trusted that he could do something to help them. But they did not yet have the faith *of* Jesus. They did not share his settled conviction that they were safe in God's hands.

This is what Paul called "the peace of Christ."

What would my life look like if I lived in the settled conviction that because of God's character and competence this world is a perfectly safe place for me to be?

- My anxiety level would go down. I would have the settled trust that my life is perfectly at rest in the hands of God. I would not be tormented by my own inadequacy.

- I would be an unhurried person. I might be busy, I might have many things to do, but I would have an inner calmness and poise that comes from being in the presence of God. I would not say so many of the foolish things I now say because I speak without thinking.
- I would not be defeated by guilt. I would live in the confidence that comes from the assurance of God's love.
- I would trust God enough to risk obeying him. I wouldn't have to hoard. Worry makes me focus on myself. It robs me of joy, energy, and compassion.

A person in whom the peace of Christ reigns would be an oasis of sanity in a world of pandemonium.

A community in which the peace of Christ reigns would change the world.

FREE TO RISK

Jesus does not offer this assurance primarily so that we can luxuriate in a sense of comfort and safety. This is not a "spirituality of the womb." The womb may be comfortable and reassuring, but it puts severe restrictions on growth.

We want safety, but we want *more* than safety. We know that if our life is dominated by the search for absolute safety we will stagnate and die. We need to grow and explore to be fully alive. In fact, comfort can be more fatal than danger. We watch scary movies and ride on roller coasters and go bungie-jumping (at least, some of us do) because we know if there is no risk in our lives we are, in a sense, already dead.

All creatures seem to have a need or a drive for growth and mastery, often in opposition to the need for safety. Years ago a Berkeley psychology student took a rat into the university's empty football stadium and opened the cage door. The first day of this experiment the rat stayed in the cage thirty minutes, poked his head out for a few seconds, then retreated. The second day, the rat ventured out a few feet. After a month of this, the rat was running all the way down the steps, across the field, up the opposite bleachers, and back home again — all without any obvious reinforcement.

> You too are in
> the watch-care
> of a great
> big God.

We flee pain and fear death, but we know that life involves more than avoiding death. So the Scriptures alternate between calls to hair-raising risks and assurances of impregnable security. And when we look at the lives of great followers of God, we see this combination of breath-taking risks with an almost brazen confidence of being safe in God's hands. Assurances of God's protection generally come in Scripture as jolts to get frightened people to risk obeying God when it feels *unsafe*. Like a father coaxing a panicky two-year-old to jump into his arms at the swimming pool: "You can trust me. I won't drop you. The pool is a perfectly safe place for you to be."

But the child will never know if she doesn't jump. The father cannot take that step for her. If she is simply grabbed and carried into the pool she never makes the choice, never exercises her own courage. She must take the leap of faith for herself.

So God coaxes his anxious "two-year-olds":

- You can defy Pharaoh.
- You can occupy the Promised Land.
- You can stand up to Goliath.
- You can give all you possess to the poor and join my rag-tag band of followers.
- You can sit in a Roman prison and face imminent execution.

All of these apparently high-risk ventures turn out to be perfectly safe places to be. You too are in the watch-care of a great big God. His arms are very strong. He has not dropped anybody yet. He will not drop you.

But you will have to trust him. You will have to jump.

How do you take that leap of trust?

One way (that is not an option for Christ-followers) is to try to make my primary goal living in peaceful, comfortable circumstances. *Time* magazine devoted a recent cover story to a current lifestyle trend: a return to small towns. People are fleeing the city with its problems, its poor and uneducated, to find a safe, quiet, comfortable place to live.

That was not the kind of peace Jesus knew. Instead, he knew trouble. John tells us that when Jesus saw the mourning at the death of Lazarus "he was deeply moved in spirit, and troubled." Before his own trial, John says Jesus was deeply troubled and testified, "I tell you the truth, one of you is going to betray me."

Because Jesus loved Lazarus he was troubled in the face of the awfulness of death. Because he loved Judas he was troubled in the face of Judas' betrayal and spiritual death.

> Don't think the peace to which we're called is a search for comfortable circumstances.

Paul, too, knew that the peace of Christ was not a free pass to escape deep trouble and concern. He coexisted not only with outer suffering but also inner turmoil: "Besides everything else, I face daily the pressure of my concern for all the churches. Who is weak, and I do not feel weak? Who is led into sin, and I do not inwardly burn?"

You know about this. You raise children and hope desperately they will live wisely and well. Sometimes your heart will be troubled. You go to the city to care for the homeless and poor, or you pray for seeking friends that are lost and hostile to God and resist him for months or years — you will know a troubled heart.

Don't think the peace to which we're called is a search for comfortable circumstances.

A WAY OF THINKING

Living in Jesus' peace means I must come to think about and see the world as Jesus himself did. I must "let the word of Christ dwell in you richly," as Paul puts it. And fundamental to Jesus' message was his insistence that right here in my world I am the object of God's unceasing vigilance.

Jesus never grew tired of teaching about this. "Why do you worry about your life, what to eat or wear?" he would ask.

"Consider the lilies of field. They neither toil nor spin." They form no floral unions, they operate without strategic plans, they never restructure. They attend no motivational seminars on how to release the redwood sleeping within them. Yet next to them Solomon himself looks like he bought his clothes at the WisePenny Thrift Shop. If God showers such beauty on grass that is here today and gone tomorrow — will he not much more clothe you? You are his beloved.

"Consider the birds of the air," Jesus said. They are not generally Type-A creatures. They don't have ulcers or high blood pressure or colitis. But they are fed by the hand of God.

Some time ago my wife and I were watching two geese and their goslings eat. One adult and nine little goslings were devouring grass, while the other adult stood guard duty.

"Look at that mother goose watch over her family," Nancy said.

"How do you know it's the mother?" I asked. "Maybe it's the father goose."

"No, it's always the mother who sacrifices herself for the family, while the father stuffs his face right along with the children. It's the same in every species."

Just then, the two adults traded off. The eater started watching, and the watcher started eating.

I was so grateful to God.

Jesus said any time you see a bird nibble some seeds you are not watching a random event, you are watching Love himself at work. Watching a bird eat is such an ordinary event that generally we don't even notice. But it's no accident that the food is available. Every time you wake up, think a thought, enjoy a meal, these are not random occurrences. They are Post-It notes of love that the Father keeps attaching to all creation, in the hopes that someone will read them.

> They are Post-It notes of love that the Father keeps attaching to all creation, in the hopes that someone will read them.

"Peace I leave with you; my peace I give to you. I do not give to you as the world gives. Do not let your hearts be troubled, and do not let them be afraid."

You have experienced this same care in your life.

There was a time when you were lonely and God sent you a friend.

There was a time you needed wisdom and guidance and it came in the form of a book or a tape or a message or wise words given at just the right time.

You were discouraged and God gave you a time of worship that flooded you with hope and courage.

You were tempted but felt a tug restraining you, and you came to your senses and pulled back from something that would have been incredibly destructive.

A WAY OF SINGING

From the beginning, the faith of the people of Israel, the faith of the people of the church, has been a faith that is expressed and strengthened in song. We are a people who sing our faith. Even those of us who can't sing well. Somehow when we sing, the words have a way of getting from our head to our heart.

Singing frames the life of Christ, from the story of his birth when Mary and Zechariah and the angels keep breaking into song, to the very end when he and his closest friends ended the Last Supper by singing a hymn before Jesus went out to die.

Singing can strengthen the soul. The book of Acts tells us that Paul and Silas had been unjustly tried, convicted, attacked by a crowd, stripped of their clothing, beaten by rods, thrown into jail, placed in an innermost cell, and fastened in stocks. Then the passage says, "About midnight Paul and Silas were praying and *singing hymns to God*, and the prisoners were listening to them" (as if they had something else to do!).

How could they sing hymns in prison? Because they were convinced that — given the magnificent God to whom they sang — it was a perfectly safe place for them to be.

It is impossible to read the Psalms — even casually — without being struck by how singing was for the psalmist both an expression of faith and a vehicle through which faith is strengthened. To sing is virtually synonymous with trusting. "But I trust in your unfailing love. . . I will sing to the LORD." God is the one who gives a song "in the night" — when it seems like there's not much worth singing about: "You turned my wailing into dancing; you removed my sackcloth and clothed me with joy, that my heart may sing to you and not be silent."

So singing became a vital part of the new community of the church. "Sing psalms, hymns, and spiritual songs with gratitude in your hearts to God," Paul says. Augustine wrote somewhere that when we sing to God, we pray twice — once in the words, but at another level in the music of the heart.

Some of our most tender moments with God are marked by song: at the funeral of someone we love, when we testify in song that death will not have the final word; during a moment in worship when nothing short of music can allow the human spirit to soar; during a time of commitment when we need to give voice to a solemn vow to follow God.

In our singing we are reminded it can be "well with our souls" even when all is wrong around us. We're reminded that this universe is a very safe place for us to be.

A WAY OF PRAYING

We begin to pursue the peace of Christ when we practice a form of prayer that is sometimes called "constantly casting": "Cast all your anxiety on him, because he cares for you." Fling them away to God, Peter says, as you would bail water out of a leaky ship.

Psychologists speak of how important it is for an infant to learn to be *alone in the presence of the parent*, especially the mother. When a child is convinced that the mother is available, attentive, and trustworthy and that he won't be abandoned, then he is no longer anxious or clinging. The child does not need to be constantly touching or even seeing the mother. He has learned to trust. In a sense, the parent is present even when the child is alone, so aloneness is no longer terrifying. He is able to explore his world with confidence.

Similarly, in prayer we learn to be *alone in the presence of God*. We speak freely to him of all our concerns and worries. We come to trust that we have not been abandoned, even if we cannot touch or see him. He is with us even when — especially when — we are alone. So aloneness is no longer terrifying. This is behind the beautiful name of the Old Testament, "Emanuel," God with us.

We must learn to cast off our anxieties, because we have so many of them. The world destroys spiritual life by generating constant anxiety. Jesus said in one of his parables that the life of the gospel is choked out by the "cares [anxieties] of this world."

We know this to be true. Yet we are more chained and tethered to the world than ever before in the history of the human race. We are much more adept at being connected to the world twenty-four hours a day than to God.

We have cable and satellite and Fed-Ex and cell phones and portable faxes and beepers and pagers and e-mail. Nothing is necessarily wrong with this technology, but we become addicted to it, slaves to it.

Richard Swenson, author of the book *Margin,* spoke of one man in California who returned home from vacation to find he had 1,000 e-mail messages. (He suggested that for many of us the greatest gift we could receive would be a "phone-less cord.")

What we need is twenty-four-hour-a-day access to God.

There is a close connection between anxiety and prayer. We see the same thing when Paul says, "Do not be anxious about anything, but in everything, by prayer and petition, with thanksgiving, present your requests to God."

Many times anxious people read words like this and feel more anxious because they worry too much. But you can't make anxiety go away by an act of the will.

The idea is to allow anxiety to become a cue for prayer. Use anxiety to strengthen your prayer.

Just as Pavlov's dogs became conditioned to salivate for dinner every time they heard the bell, we can use anxiety to become a cue for prayer. Don't worry about how much anxiety you feel. Simply direct your anxiety toward God.

The anxious feelings may subside. They may not. Don't beat yourself up about that. Your job is not to make sure your feelings are "spiritually correct."

Your job — and mine — is to practice constant casting.

You can start right now. Think of the greatest burden on your mind. Maybe it's a problem where you lack wisdom, guilt that plagues you, a task that overwhelms you, a loss or disappointment that seems too much to bear.

You have been carrying it by yourself. Cast it on God.

A NEW WAY OF FEELING

A friend of mine was putting his five-year-old daughter to bed. An hour after he had completed tuck-in he returned to check on her, and to his surprise she was still wide awake.

"What are you doing?" he asked.

"Thinking."

"About what?"

"I was thinking about being a bride," she said. "Someday, I'm going to be a bride, you know. I'm going to have a wedding, I'm going to wear the special dress. And you, Daddy, will be my prince."

In her mind, the whole business of brides and princesses and grooms and princes was somehow all mixed together. She would be the Princess Bride.

"That's wonderful, honey, but I can't be your prince."

"Why not?" she huffed, seriously put out by this news.

So my friend had to explain that he already was Mommy's prince and that society would frown on that sort of thing.

> This cry of our heart to be loved is only the faint echo of God's desire to love us.

"Well, then who *will* be my prince?" she wanted to know.

"I don't know. Maybe Aaron or Brandon or any one of the boys you know. But maybe not. Probably, you don't even know him yet. In fact, the wisest thing to do is, when it comes time to choose the Prince, let Daddy decide. Don't do anything Prince-wise without checking with Daddy first."

There is in every human heart an inextinguishable desire to be someone's prince, someone's princess. We want to be beloved.

The Bible says we are. The writers of Scripture use the most extravagant images available to convince us of this. God's love for us is the love of a friend who would sacrifice his life for the one he loves, the love of a father for a runaway son, the love of a mother that will not allow her to forget her child. God's love for us is more passionate than the heart of the most passionate groom for his bride.

You are the beloved of God.

This cry of our heart to be loved is only the faint echo of God's desire to love us. Before you were ever born, you were beloved in the mind of God. This is the deepest secret to your identity. It cannot be earned or won, only gratefully embraced.

> We spend our lives trying to earn the love that we can only receive when we admit our poverty of spirit.

Nothing you will ever do could make God love you more than he does right now: not greater achievement, not greater beauty, not wider recognition, not even greater levels of spirituality and obedience.

Nothing you have ever done could make God love you any less: not any sin, not any failure, not any guilt, not any regret.

The irony is we spend our lives trying to earn the love that we can only receive when we admit our poverty of spirit.

"See what love the Father has given us, that we should be called children of God; and that is what we are." John says.

To learn to live in the love of God is the challenge of a lifetime. Martin Luther wrote, "This is the ineffable and infinite mercy of God which the slender capacity of man's heart cannot comprehend and much less utter — the unfathomable depth and burning zeal of God's love toward us."

CREATING SAFE PLACES FOR OTHERS

When we know ourselves to be safe with God, we can begin to create havens of safety for others.

Several years ago a friend of mine in Chicago began what's called the Emmaeus ministry. The people they are trying to help are young men in their late teens or early twenties who come to Chicago, having no families — in fact, they almost never even know who their fathers are. They are trapped in drug abuse and end up surviving by becoming street hustlers — male prostitutes. This is not a group to whom many people are likely to extend love.

So these people with Emmaeus simply walk the streets of Chicago from ten until two or three in the morning, looking for the most ragged of rag dolls. Every once in a while some man trapped in hustling will say, "I can't take it anymore. Is there any way out of this hell?" And then John and his friends will offer shelter or training and try to help him find the way.

John was sitting in his living room one night with a young man named Joseph. John's wife and some other members of their little community were setting the table, and they invited Joseph to have dinner with them. Joseph whispered to John as they sat down, "I've never done this before." John was confused. "Done what?"

"This family dinner thing around a table. I've never done that."

Joseph was typical of the young men in his world. He didn't know his father, his mother was a crack addict and abusive, he was removed from his home when he was four months old. He had been shuttled from group home to group home in the child-care system. He was in a gang by age eleven, in prison by sixteen. Now he was in his midtwenties and never once in his life had he sat down to eat a meal around a table with a real family. Never had he participated as a father and mother and children passed the food and looked each other in the eye and talked about their day.

He was embarrassed. "I've never done this, but I've seen it on TV."

Who is going to tell him that he is not alone? Who is going to tell Joseph that he, too, is beloved of God?

In Twelve-Step groups people often introduce themselves by saying, "My name is John. I'm an alcoholic." It is a way of breaking through denial and embracing the truth of brokenness. It has been suggested that in the church we ought to greet each other by saying, "My name is John. I'm a sinner." Probably not a bad idea. Certainly I know what it is to spend enormous amounts of time and energy trying to convince people I'm better than I am. "My name is John. I'm a sinner." I need to say that.

But there are other words I need to hear and speak. In some ways, they are even more embarrassing to say. Perhaps even harder to believe. They are these words: "My name is John. I am the beloved. I am loved by God."

You and I need these words. It may be that you can't say those words without laughing, or perhaps you can't say them without crying.

One of the most beautiful passages in Scripture is found in Isaiah 43. God is speaking to his people, and although the words are addressed to Israel they are yours and mine as well. Read them, and allow them to be God's word to you.

> I have called you by name, you are mine.
> When you pass through the waters, I will be with you;
>   and through the rivers, they shall not overwhelm you;
> when you walk through fire you shall not be burned,
>   and the flame shall not consume you,
> [for God is a great big God,
> though you can't see him or hear him,
> he is always with you.
> He never takes his eye off you].
> For I am the LORD your God,
>   the Holy One of Israel, your Savior. . .
> Because you are precious in my sight,
>   and honored, and I love you.

Perhaps you could write down that last phrase on a card and carry it with you: "For you are precious in my sight, and honored, and I love you."

You are the beloved of God. What more do you need to achieve or prove or acquire? You are the beloved of God. Who else do you need to impress? What other ladder do you need to climb?

You are the beloved of God. What are you going to add to your resumé that is going to top that?

What if you were to make your life an experiment of living in the love of God? Every morning, when you wake up, let your first words be "I am the beloved." Each night, when you go to sleep, let your last words echo, "I am the beloved."

Write those words down, and carry them with you. When you're tempted to despair because you've blown it, take out the card and look at it. When you wake up and you're tempted to be overwhelmed by all you have to do, take it out and look at it.

Take it out when you are tempted to sin, to dishonor God; when you are tempted to lash out in anger and hurt someone, or deceive someone, or use someone; when you're afraid; when you're anxious; when you're alone. Remember and feast on the words that give life.

The God who loves you is greater than you can imagine. You may not be able to see him or hear him, but he is here. He is watching.

Big paws. Fierce growl.

"For you are precious in my sight, and honored, and I love you."

ELEVEN

GOD SEARCHES
FOR HIDING PEOPLE

*So God hides himself in order to raise souls up to that perfect
faith which will discover him under every kind of disguise.
For once they knew God's secret, disguise is useless. They say:
"See him! There he is, behind the wall, looking through the
trellis, in at the window!" O divine Love, conceal yourself,
leap over our suffering, make us obedient. Mystify us, arouse
and confuse us. Shatter all our illusions and plans so that we
lose our way, and see neither path nor light until we have
found you. . . For how foolish it is, O Divine Love, not to see you
in all that is good and in all creatures.*

JEAN PIERRE DE CAUSSADE

The way to love anything is to realize that it might be lost.

G. K. CHESTERTON

Our loving God, Jesus once said, is like a shepherd who can't
stop searching for one lamb even though you'd think he'd be
satisfied with the ninety-nine he already has. We keep on hiding,
but he can't seem to stop seeking.

Robert Fulghum wrote about sitting in his office and listening
to the neighborhood kids playing hide-and-seek. He remembered
playing as a child. He remembered especially one kid who hid too
well. Eventually the other kids would give up seeking — leading

to fights about the true nature of the game: hiding and seeking and bickering.

There was a boy outside Fulghum's office who was hiding too well and was about to be abandoned. Fulghum thought about yelling, "Get found, kid!" but decided it would probably cause too much trouble.

Adults, too, he noted, have a tendency to hide too well. We cover up our faults and flaws and fears, then wonder why we feel so abandoned and alone.

"Wanting to hide. Needing to be sought. Confused about being found" — not a bad diagnosis of the human condition.

Fulghum notes that God himself has been written about in the language of hide-and-seek. *Deus Absconditus* is the old term for this: the God who hides himself.

But Fulghum says his guess is that God is into finding, not hiding — that he prefers a game called Sardines, in which the person who is It hides, and everyone looks for him, and when you find him, you hide next to him until everybody is hiding together and giggling so loud that their location is no longer a secret.

"I think old God is a Sardine player. And will be found in the same way everyone else gets found in Sardines — by the laughter of those heaped together at the end."

The Bible says, "They heard the sound of the LORD God walking in the garden at the time of the evening breeze, and the man and his wife hid themselves from the presence of the LORD God among the trees of the garden. But the LORD God called to the man, and said to him, 'Where are you?' He said, 'I heard the sound of you in the garden, and I was afraid, because I was naked, and I hid myself.' "

WANTING TO HIDE. NEEDING TO BE SOUGHT. CONFUSED ABOUT BEING FOUND.

Hide-and-seek is a simple game. One person seeks, everyone else hides. Hence the name. It is most fun for those who hide.

When you hide, you choose where you go. When you hide, you get to keep your eyes open. Those who hide are in control. Everyone wants to hide.

The hard job is to be the seeker. The seeker deliberately allows those who hide to get away. The seeker places herself in the humble position of searching on and on for people who deliberately evade her, who laugh at her. No one wants to be the seeker.

The one who searches does not even get much of a title. In other games, the pivotal player at least gets a high-profile name — the center, the pitcher, the goalkeeper. The one who searches is simply called IT. Not Captain IT, not Chief Executive IT, just IT. In fact, the call that starts the game is simply "not IT."

Whoever is IT will have to be very patient. IT will have to search long and hard. IT will have to face evasion and trickery.

At the end of the game, if someone hides too well, IT will yell the words that end the game. IT cups ITs hands and hollers so that the cry can be heard through the whole neighborhood: "Olly-olly-oxen-free!"

No one knows quite where this chant came from, or what it originally meant. (Latin, perhaps, for "liberate the oxen"?) But hiders know what it means. You can come home. You're safe. You will not be chased or hurt or penalized. You can return — like the prodigal son coming home to the fatted calf. Stop hiding. Come home. It is a cry of grace.

The story of God and the human race is a story of hide-and-seek. Only we get confused sometimes about who is IT.

A bumper sticker that was popular years ago in some church circles proclaimed "I FOUND IT." In a strict theological sense, the slogan is backwards. The truth is, IT found me.

Often those of us on a spiritual journey think of ourselves as searchers. And of course there is a certain truth to this. We ask questions, read books, attend classes, look for truth that often seems elusive. We search for God. The writers of Scripture commend this: "You will seek me, and find me when you seek me with all your heart," God says.

But that is not the whole story. I'm not just a searcher. I'm also a hider. You too. We have to come face-to-face with our tendency to hide, to get lost.

Wanting to Hide

I fled him, down the nights and down the days;
I fled him, down the arches of the years;
I fled him, down the labyrinthine ways of my own mind;
and in the mist of tears I hid from him,
and under running laughter.

Hiddenness is always the first response to an awareness that I have sinned. So writes Francis Thompson in the magnificent poem "The Hound of Heaven." I hide from God in moments that stretch into decades. I hide through my rationalizations and denials — the "labyrinthine ways of my own mind." I hide despite the tears and the laughter that would lead me back to him if I would only let them.

This has been the flight of the human race since the Garden. Human beings were not made to hide. From the beginning our great craving was to know and be known. This is the significance of the statement in Genesis about Adam and Eve: "They were naked, and they were not ashamed." No hiddenness. No reason to hide. Full knowing.

With sin this was lost. After the Fall, when God came to be with Adam, Adam's response was that he had heard God in the garden, and he was afraid, since he realized he was naked, "so [he] hid."

This is my story. I hide because I don't want to be exposed in my fallenness, my darkness. I hide because I'm afraid if the truth about me is known, I will never be loved. I hide from other people. I hide from God. I hide from truth — in a sense, I hide even from myself.

Sin and hiding are inseparable, the Siamese twins of the fallen soul. At one point in his life my younger brother Bart decided he wanted constant access to the cookie jar. He wanted this even though my mother had made it clear that it was the one forbidden source of food in the kitchen. From every vegetable bin and fruit bowl we could freely eat, but the Jar of the Knowledge of Good and Evil meant death.

But Bart operated on the belief (psychologists say it is a common one at a certain developmental stage) that as long as *he* couldn't see anything, no one else could see anything either. So he would walk into the kitchen, squeeze his eyelids shut and clamp one hand over them just to be on the safe side. *Bartus Absconditus*. He would inch across the floor, his free hand groping cupboard handles and counter space, until he identified the cookie jar. He would remove the lid, liberate the cookies, and inch backward out of the kitchen without ever having opened his eyes. And my parents would be laughing so hard they never did anything to stop him. (I did not think it was very funny, though, particularly because he was seventeen years old at the time. . . .)

The irony is that I hide because I'm afraid that if the full truth about me is known I won't be loved. But whatever is *hidden* cannot be *loved*. I can only be loved to the extent that I am known. I can only be *fully* loved if I am *fully* known.

When I hide parts of myself, I seek to convince another person I am better than I am. If I'm a good enough hider, I may get away with it. The other person may express affection and love for me. But always comes the voice inside me: *Yes, but if you knew the truth about me, if you saw the hidden places, you would not love me. You love the person you think I am. You do not love the real me, for you do not know the real me.*

Adam was doing pretty much the same thing. But perhaps the most surprising part of the story is the role God plays. When he enters the garden he asks a question: "Adam, where are you?"

Why should God ask that question? Is the omniscient one confused? Is God really at a loss as to Adam's whereabouts? For years I read that question without noticing its significance.

> The kind of presence God desires cannot be coerced, not even by God.

This is one of the most remarkable questions in Scripture. God is allowing Adam to hide from him. The kind of presence God desires cannot be coerced, not even by God. It must be offered from a willing heart. God grants to his creatures the freedom to be known or to be unknown by him. God covers his eyes.

But there's more to it than that. God doesn't just allow Adam to hide. God comes searching for him. God takes the initiative to restore their closeness, even though Adam is the one withholding himself. After he finishes counting to one hundred, God says, "I'll be IT."

"All we like sheep have gone astray," says the prophet Isaiah. Who hides? The man who knows he needs to change his priorities, whose kids don't know him, who can't remember the last time he prayed in a meaningful way, whose every act is calculated to advance his success but who is so addicted to it that he refuses to see the truth or to allow others to see it — he's hiding.

Who hides? The woman who is filled with anger at her mother or her husband or her children, or at God because she does not have a husband or does not have the husband she wants. But hers is a frozen anger. She does not acknowledge it even to herself. It just leaks out of her and corrodes her relationships and her heart — she's hiding.

The couple who have attended church for years, whose life is friendly and respectable but whose marriage is dead, they have not known emotional intimacy for years, have not made love or laughed together for longer than they can remember — they're hiding.

We use language to help us hide. Abusers acknowledge only being "impatient" with their children because they have been driven to distraction. Self-serving flattery is labeled affirmation; gossip is offered under the guise of helping another to "pray more intelligently." Sexual promiscuity, as long as the partners are entertained one at a time, is christened "serial monogamy"; greedy financial decisions are justified as "doing what's right for my family"; lazy persons are labeled "motivationally dispossessed"; and prostitutes called "sex care providers."

Needing to Be Sought

Up vistaed hopes I sped . . .
From those strong Feet that followed, followed after.
But with unhurrying chase,
And unperturbed pace,
Deliberate speed, majestic instancy,
They beat — and a Voice beat
More instant than the Feet —
"All things betray thee, who betrayest Me."

FRANCIS THOMPSON, THE HOUND OF HEAVEN

I hide and evade, but God is the one who seeks — unhurrying, unperturbed, refusing to stop — the hound of heaven.

In Jesus' story of the lost sheep, an animal is lost and is unable to make its way home by itself. The sheep is not a bright animal. We all know that animals with any intelligence eventually get a TV show of their own: dolphins had Flipper, cats have Garfield, dogs and horses have had too many to mention, even pigs had the character Arnold on the television program *Green Acres*. But celebrated sheep are hard to come by.

Sheep are notorious creatures of habit. Left to themselves they will follow a trail until it becomes a rut, graze hills until they turn into desert wastelands, pollute the ground from which they feed until it is corrupt with disease and parasites.

Sheep are not proactive animals. Sheep are followers. If one sheep goes over a cliff, a whole flock could follow. You'd think somewhere along the line one sheep would notice, would stop and think, *Hmmm. Sally went over the edge and never came back. I'll think I'll pause a moment and reflect on this course before I impulsively plunge ahead.*

This never happens. Sheep just think, *Well, okay, I guess I'll give it a try. Doesn't sound like a ba-a-a-d idea to me.*

Shepherds speak of "cast" sheep; their term for a sheep that gets turned on its back and becomes helpless. Shepherd-author Philip Keller explains,

> The way it happens is this. A heavy, fat, or long-fleeced sheep will lie down comfortably in some little hollow or depression in the ground. It may roll on its side slightly to stretch out or relax. Suddenly the center of gravity in the body shifts so that it turns on its back far enough that the feet no longer touch the ground. It may feel a sense of panic and start to paw frantically. Frequently this only makes things worse. It rolls over even further. Now it is quite impossible for it to regain its feet.
>
> As it lies there struggling, gases begin to build up in the rumen [the sheep's first stomach]. As these expand they tend to retard and cut off blood circulation to extremities of the body, especially the legs. If the weather is very hot and sunny a cast sheep can die in a few hours.

I hide and evade, but God is the one who seeks — unhurrying, unperturbed, refusing to stop — the hound of heaven.

I cannot make it out of hiding on my own. I need to be sought. Most often in this life this seeking takes the form of someone loving me in the name of God, even when they see the ugliness I try to hide.

One night at home not long ago I came downstairs. Nancy had been working in the kitchen. I'd been upstairs, probably vacuuming or something.

Nancy asked, "Would you help me unload the dishwasher?"

Certainly. I'm a servant. We'll do it in community.

After doing this with me for a few minutes, she started making entries in the checkbook.

This registered with me, though the process was so subtle, I was hardly even aware what I was thinking: *If she's going to get off at this exit, I'm going to get off at this exit.*

So I started making coffee for the next morning: I drink coffee, she doesn't.

Nancy said, "Are you making coffee?" (You will understand she was not looking for verbal verification here. The correct response was not "Yes, I'm making a delicious hot beverage for tomorrow.")

So I said, "Well, you stopped first to work on the checkbook."

"Ah, but the checkbook is for both of us, the coffee is just for you."

This was true, but the subtlety of the point escaped me.

This led to a fascinating discussion about division of labor issues, the Bible and gender roles, the relative functional level of our families of origin, and absorbing insights into each other's mothers.

When we had finished and reached resolution, I noticed a strange thing. Nancy was ready to resume closeness, but I found myself wanting to withdraw from her.

Here's part of what was going on in my mind: *I'll withdraw and be a victim. Go ahead, put the load on me. Lincoln freed the slaves — all but one. When she sees how miserable and sad and morally superior I am, she'll feel awful. Then she'll do what I want her to do. I can control and manipulate by strategic hiding.*

It's not working real well so far.

Hiding becomes for me not just a way of avoiding pain and embarrassment, it also becomes a way to punish the one I know wants to be in community with me.

When can I get the courage to stop hiding? When I am loved. In *Phantom of the Opera*, the phantom wears a mask to hide his horribly disfigured face. He lives in the bowels of the old opera house, to cloak his presence and bitter misdeeds. But the woman Christine touches his heart. At the climax of the story, his mask is removed. In that moment he chooses to be known, to be seen. He knows that his face is hideous; he waits for her to scream in terror, but she does not. Her heart is moved by compassion and pity. She does not turn away. She gently kisses his scarred face.

> First the mask must come off. Then love can penetrate the heart.

And her love changes him, at least a little. He is able to let her go, to give her her freedom, even though he knows it is the end of his dream. When he was able to stop hiding for a moment, he could be known and loved as he was, even in all his disfigurement. First the mask must come off. Then love can penetrate the heart.

Confused About Being Found

Halts by me that footfall;
Is my gloom, after all,
Shade of His hand, outstretched caressingly?
"Ah, fondest, blindest, weakest,
I am He whom thou seekest!
Thou longeth love from me, who longs for thee."

FRANCIS THOMPSON, *THE HOUND OF HEAVEN*

Luke tells the story of one wretched hider named Zacchaeus, a tax collector.

In Israel, certain vocations carried a heavy social stigma. They were called "despised trades," and no devout Jewish person would engage in them. Religious leaders would make lists of these despised trades and warn the people to choose a different career.

Some occupations make only a few lists. One of the lists has at the bottom physicians and butchers (because they're tempted to cater to the rich and be unfair to the poor) and comments, "The best among physicians is destined for hell, and the most seemly of butchers is a partner of evil."

Some occupations are listed not because they are dishonorable but just because they are repugnant. One of the lists had tanner of dead skins and dung-collector. Dung collecting was actually a career choice. If a woman's husband became a dung-collector she actually had the right to divorce him and receive a sum of money. Even if she married him knowing he was going into that profession — in the words of one rabbi, she could say, "I thought I could endure it, but I cannot."

There were a few professions, however, that were not merely unpleasant but were considered immoral. People who practiced these were not only considered unpleasant to be around, they were to be shunned. Here's one such list:

Gambler with dice
Usurer (because they were thought to exploit the poor)
Pigeon-trainer (nothing against pigeons — pigeon racing is a form of gambling)
Tax collector

Israel was occupied by Rome, and Rome was primarily interested in how much money they could wring out of the country. So instead of having Romans collect taxes, they would get Israelites to do it.

They would let people bid for the right to be a tax collector for a particular area. The highest bidder got the job. He could collect as much in taxes as he could get away with. He had to give to Rome what he had bid — whatever was left over, he would keep.

So tax collectors were despised as traitors who had sold out their brothers and sisters to their enemy for a profit. It was just assumed any tax collector was guilty of massive dishonesty. There was a saying: "for tax collectors, repentance is hard," because tax collectors had cheated so many people they wouldn't even know to whom they should go back and make amends. One Roman writer wrote about a town that erected a statue to an honest tax collector.

They were not only hated, tax collectors were deprived of their political and civil rights. They could not serve as a witness in the courts, and they were not allowed to serve as judges. A devout Israelite would not even allow the hem of his robe to touch the robe of a tax collector.

If you want to get a feel for it, think in terms of the most despised categories in our society. Drug dealer. Mafia hit man.

What made Zacchaeus willing to enter a profession that would make him hated?

We don't know much about Zacchaeus, other than that he had one prominent physical characteristic. For a man to be considered attractive, he is supposed to have three traits: tall, dark, and handsome. Zacchaeus may have had two of the three, but he was vertically challenged. He was, in the words of the old Sunday school song, "a wee little man."

Maybe Zacchaeus decided he would show them all and become a big man in the only way he knew how. Money became the guiding force of his life.

In any event, he became a tax collector, and he was good at it. He was the chief tax collector — had others working for him. And he was rich. It's fair to assume he was thoroughly corrupt. He had given up on society, on friendships, on decency — he was betting everything he had that affluence and wealth were what would give meaning and fulfillment to his life.

It wasn't working. The possessions, wealth, security, and power for which he had sold his soul were not paying off. *All things betray thee, who betrayest Me.* Something about Jesus intrigued him. It's not hard to figure out what it was.

Luke's gospel tells us that Jesus sought out a tax collector to become one of his followers and friends. Not only that, Levi — a tax collector (also known as Matthew) who had become one of Jesus' disciples — threw a party for his IRS friends, and Jesus went to it. The religious leaders challenged him on this: "Why do you eat and drink with tax collectors?"

Word about something like this gets around. Jesus goes to parties for tax collectors. One of his followers is a former tax collector himself. Zacchaeus wants to see this man who hangs around with people like him.

Zacchaeus wants to see Jesus, but there's a crowd. When you're a tax collector, you're not a popular guy in a crowd. People are not likely to make way for a little tax collector to be able to see. There's liable to be a fair amount of shoving and pushing and cursing for any tax collector who would be foolish enough just to show up.

So he climbs up into a tree. He climbs up to see over the crowd. But it may be that he climbs also to hide. Knowing and being known is his greatest longing and his greatest fear.

Jesus draws closer, and Zacchaeus is pleased that he'll get such a good look.

Then he's not only close, he's standing right beside the tree; he's looking up into the tree. The whole crowd, hundreds of people, is looking up into the tree with him.

"What's he looking at?"

"I don't know; looks like there's some kid up there."

Jesus says, "Zacchaeus." One word, and it sets off a buzz through the crowd.

Imagine how Zacchaeus feels. He thinks he's going to hide in a tree, watch from a safe distance, and all of a sudden Jesus and everybody he knows is looking at him up a tree.

"Zacchaeus." The crowd is straining to see a corrupt, traitorous tax collector get what's coming to him.

"Zacchaeus," Jesus says, "will you get out of the tree? It's hard to carry on a serious conversation this way. Hurry down."

And then the words for which no one was prepared, Zacchaeus least of all: "I *must* stay at your house today."

> The human heart can't deal with the guilt of secret shame.

Think of such a person in your mind, whom all polite and decent people would shun. Then imagine Jesus walking up to him and treating him with courtesy and dignity — of not only touching him but asking to go to his home and sit down and eat with him — and you may get some sense of the shock and confusion everybody felt. And Zacchaeus does it. He comes out of the tree.

He finally acknowledges the truth: his whole life has been built on greed and dishonesty. He has sinned against his God and his people. He comes out of hiding.

Time magazine profiled a new phone service some time ago. It was an "apology sound off line," a service that would receive two hundred phone calls a day from people who call up just to get something off their chest. It has featured confessions of everything from marital infidelity to murder.

They have a second number — more costly — that people can dial and pay to listen to confessions. They have received up to 10,000 calls a day.

Why would people pay to call up and confess? Because the human heart can't deal with the guilt of secret shame. It's the one place they know they can confess their guilt with a guarantee they will not be judged. They crave some relief from the truth about themselves.

Imagine that instead of Zacchaeus, it's you up in the tree. You long to see Jesus, and yet part of you is afraid to see Jesus, because you know your life doesn't quite measure up. Imagine you are in the tree, half hoping Jesus will see you and half hoping he won't. If Jesus were to come along today and see you up in the tree, what would he need to talk to you about? What is it in your life you are most apt to hide?

Part of our raggedness is that we're willing to live with huge problems as long as other people don't find out about them.

When I used to leave home to go out somewhere, my mother always wanted to know if I had on clean clothes: not just outer clothes but also undershirt and socks and things you don't see. Why? Not because it would feel good or because it would promote health and good hygiene, but in case I got in an accident.

She wasn't worried about the accident. She just wanted to make sure that when the police came if I'd been maimed, disfigured, or paralyzed at least they wouldn't think my mom let me leave the house in dirty underwear.

(For a long time I figured that's the first thing police checked at accidents: "It's pretty bad; I'm not sure he'll make it." "Okay. Better check his underwear, find out what kind of a mother this man had.")

Notice Jesus' approach. We might expect him to say something like "Zacchaeus, if you'll clean up your life, change professions, and pay back what you owe, I'll come to your house. I won't come now, it would look like I'm condoning what you've done. Frankly, I can't afford the criticism it would cause, but clean up your life and I'll come."

But Jesus does not say this. The Hound of Heaven insists on befriending Zacchaeus even before Zacchaeus gets respectable. Luke is quite clear about how widespread the revulsion is. "All who saw it" began to grumble, he says.

Their problem was they were more spiritual than Jesus. (It was a distorted spirituality, of course.) This is a general rule of thumb:

If you find yourself getting more spiritual than Jesus, you've gone too far.

And so Zacchaeus comes out of hiding. He says he will pay back anyone he's cheated four times the amount. By law he was only obligated to pay what he took plus a penalty of twenty percent. But he went beyond that to replace greed with generosity. And he didn't stop there. In addition to making reparations, he says he will take half of everything and simply give it away to whoever needs it.

The sign of a life that has truly been found is that the primary desire in response to wrongdoing becomes the will to set things right, insofar as it is possible. This is the difference between repentance and damage control.

The IRS has a special fund set up called a "cheater's account." The idea is to provide a service to people who have cheated on taxes and feel guilty. So people who have cheated on their taxes can send in money anonymously to make it up. The IRS is supposed to have received one letter that reads, "I have cheated on my taxes for years, and I feel so guilty I can't sleep at night. Enclosed please find a money order for $10,000. P.S.: If I still can't sleep, I'll send in the rest of what I owe."

Zacchaeus — wretched and despised as he was — was only one sincere confession away from intimacy with God. He was as lost as it was possible to be, but he was that close to life in the kingdom of God.

To all who want to hide, who need to be sought, who are confused about being found, God has spoken in Jesus Christ. "Olly-olly-oxen-free," God says. "Come out, come out, wherever you are. The time for hiding is over. The time for coming home has arrived. No penalties, no punishment, no getting caught, just come home. Trust me."

To all who have been hiding too well, too long, God says it. "Get found, kid! Come home."

TWELVE

THE RAGGED GOD

The Word became flesh and lived among us, and we have seen his glory, the glory as of a father's only son, full of grace and truth.

JOHN 1:14

"Do you know which of all the characters in the Bible is most tragic?" he asked me. "It is God, blessed be His name, God whose creatures so often disappoint and betray him."

ELIE WIESEL

Why is it that we beheld the glory of God in flesh — finite, limited, ordinary flesh? Why did God become like one of us? Why is he the God of the manger, the God of the cross?

Danish philosopher Søren Kierkegaard told a parable about why God communicated his love the way he did.

Imagine there was a king that loved a humble maiden, Kierkegaard said. She had no royal pedigree, no education, no standing in the court. She dressed in rags. She lived in a hovel. She led the ragged life of a peasant. But for reasons no one could ever quite figure out, the king fell in love with this girl, in the way kings sometimes do. Why he should love her is beyond explaining, but love her he did. And he could not stop loving her.

Then there awoke in the heart of the king an anxious thought. How was he to reveal his love to the girl? How could he bridge the chasm of station and position that separated them? His advisers, of course, would tell him to simply command her to be his queen. For he was a man of immense power — every statesman feared his wrath, every foreign power trembled before him, every courtier groveled in the dust at the king's voice. She would have no power to resist; she would owe him an eternal debt of gratitude.

But power — even unlimited power — cannot command love. He could force her body to be present in his palace; he could not force love for him to be present in her heart. He might be able to gain her obedience this way, but coerced submission is not what he wanted. He longed for intimacy of heart and oneness of spirit. All the power in the world cannot unlock the door to the human heart. It must be opened from the inside.

His advisers might suggest that the king give up this love, give his heart to a more worthy woman. But this the king will not do, cannot do. And so his love is also his pain. Kierkegaard writes, "What a depth of grief [lies] in this unhappy love. . . No human being is destined to suffer such grief. . . God has reserved it to himself, this unfathomable grief. . . For the divine love is that unfathomable love which cannot rest content."

The king could try to bridge the chasm between them by elevating her to his position. He could shower her with gifts, dress her in purple and silk, have her crowned queen. But if he brought her to his palace, if he radiated the sun of his magnificence over her, if she saw all the wealth and power and pomp of his greatness, she would be overwhelmed. How would he know (or she either, for that matter) if she loved him for himself or for all that he gave her? How could she know that he loved her and would love her still even if she had remained only a humble peasant? "Would she be able to summon confidence enough never to remember what the king wished only to forget, that he was king and she had been a humble maiden?"

Every other alternative came to nothing. There was only one way. So one day the king rose, left his throne, removed his crown, relinquished his scepter, and laid aside his royal robes. He took upon himself the life of a peasant. He dressed in rags, scratched out a living in the dirt, groveled for food, dwelt in a hovel. He did not just take on the outward appearance of a servant, it became his actual life, his nature, his burden. Kierkegaard: "But the servant-form is no mere outer garment, and therefore God must suffer all things, endure all things. . . he must be forsaken in death, absolutely like the humblest — behold the man! His suffering is not that of his death, but this entire life is a story of suffering; and it is love that suffers, the love which gives all is itself in want." He became as ragged as the one he loved, so that she could be united to him forever. It was the only way.

His raggedness became the very signature of his presence: "And this shall be a sign unto you; ye shall find the babe wrapped in swaddling clothes, lying in a manger."

"Foxes have holes, and birds of the air have nests; but the Son of Man has nowhere to lay his head."

This is the God who removed his robe and wrapped a servant's towel around himself with which to wash his disciples' feet. The God of whom it was said in Isaiah, "He had no form or majesty that we should look at him, nothing in his appearance that we should desire him." The God who at the last was mocked with and stripped of a purple robe, and crucified wearing a crown of thorns. Of all the gods of myth, literature, and religion, this alone is the Ragged God.

THE GLORY OF GOD

God came to earth. We beheld his glory. Not the glory of thrones and crowns. No, his glory was that he would lay all that aside for ragged, sin-filled, little peasants like you and me.

John writes, "No one has ever seen God." It is God the only Son, who is close to the Father's heart, who has made him known.

When the Bible says no one has ever *seen* God, it is of course not talking about physical seeing in the ordinary sense. God is not limited to a physical body; he is spirit. The idea is not that God is an elusive recluse like Howard Hughes or Greta Garbo in their later years.

The truth being expressed is that no one has ever fully *experienced* the reality of God. No one has grasped and comprehended his character and nature. We have ideas and pictures about him, but our own projections and misconceptions are always at work distorting our view of him to one degree or another. C. S. Lewis writes in *The Screwtape Letters* about the importance of remembering to pray to God "as-You-truly-are-in-Yourself," not simply "as-I-think-you-are-in-my-mind." Remembering this distinction, addressing God "as-you-truly-are-in-yourself," is the most dangerous prayer of all, he says, the prayer that the Evil One most seeks to discourage.

Perhaps the area we are most likely to get confused is when it comes to the idea of glory. Humanly speaking, glory is generally about status. Glory consists of beauty, fame, power, intelligence, achievement, and wealth. It is sought on battlefields and in boardrooms, celebrated on magazine covers and media profiles.

Consider this ad from the "Strictly Personal" section of *New York* magazine placed by a woman who, in the words of Neal Plantinga, wants to meet a man as remarkable as herself:

Strikingly Beautiful — *Ivy League graduate. Playful, passionate, perceptive, elegant, bright, articulate, original in mind, unique in spirit. I possess a rare balance of beauty and depth, sophistication and earthiness, seriousness and a love of fun. Professionally successful, perfectly capable of being self-sufficient and independent, but I won't be truly content until we find each other. Please reply with a substantial letter describing your background and who you are. Photo essential.*

I suppose it might be hard to possess a rare balance of beauty and depth and not want to let others know about it, but even so, this seems a bit intimidating. If she is unfamiliar with all the other aspects of Jesus' teaching, she certainly has got the "don't hide your light under a bushel" part down. A profile in glory, at least from a human perspective.

We run to glory, and we run from raggedness. Author Elie Wiesel writes of a time when the left side of his body was shattered in an auto accident; he required ten hours of reconstructive surgery and months of recovery. But his friends kept consoling him with the same thought: You're lucky; it could have been worse. You could have lost your sight, your legs, your mind.

> We run toward glory and away from raggedness, suffering, aloneness, pain.

It reminded him, Wiesel said, of an old story about a man reciting a litany of woes to his friend — he has lost his job, his house, his money, his fiancée — and his friend keeps saying, "It could have been worse." Finally the man screams, "How could it be worse?" and his friend mutters, "It could have happened to me."

We run toward glory and away from raggedness, suffering, aloneness, pain. "It could have been worse. It could have happened to me."

God thinks differently about glory than we do. There are hints of this in the Old Testament. The writer of Exodus tells us that after Moses pleaded with God to continue to lead Israel after the people's idolatry with the golden calf, he had one more request just for himself:

"Show me your glory, I pray."

Moses hungered for the glory of God. And God says yes. God agrees to reveal his glory to Moses.

But before we go on with the story, let's take a moment to reflect. What do you expect Moses will see? What do you think of when you hear the phrase "the glory of God"? Thunder and lightning? Earthquakes and tidal waves? A cosmic special effects show? I would have expected this to be a scene of great power. A demonstration of majesty and brilliance and force that would overwhelm this small, insignificant human creature. This is the way human beings generally think about the glory of gods — Zeus and Thor always had a few thunderbolts at hand.

"Show me your glory, I pray."

Then God answers, with words that can bring tears to your eyes when you think about them. God agrees to unveil his glory to Moses, and this is what he says: "I will make all my *goodness* pass before you."

That's it. That's the ultimate glory of God. Not his strong right arm or his terrible swift sword, though these, of course, are part of God as well. What is most glorious about God is not ultimately his power or strength or might or majesty, great though these may be. What is most glorious about God is how sheerly, unalterably *good* he is. Moses asks to see God's *glory*, and God says, "I will make all my goodness pass before you, and will proclaim before you the name, 'The LORD'; and I will be gracious to whom I will be gracious, and will show mercy on whom I will show mercy."

> What is most glorious about God is how sheerly, unalterably *good* he is.

What is most glorious about God is how sheerly good he is. Yet, for the fullest look at this the human race would have to wait for a carpenter from Galilee.

Jesus came to show us the glory of God, but it is not like human glory. It's not the kind of glory that gets named *People's* sexiest man of the year, or *Time's* man of the year, or *Forbes'* wealthiest man of the year. His glory was made most visible when he took on our raggedness.

HUMAN RAGGEDNESS

Elie Wiesel has written perhaps as hauntingly about the raggedness of life as anyone in our time. A novelist and winner of the Nobel Peace Prize, Wiesel was an adolescent survivor of the Holocaust in which he lost his father, mother, and sister. He refuses to allow us to settle for easy answers for the existence of such terrible suffering. He saw with his own eyes the black smoke unfurling in the sky from the ovens in which his mother and sister would die.

> Never shall I forget that night, the first night in camp, which has turned my life into one long night, seven times cursed and seven times sealed. Never shall I forget that smoke. Never shall I forget the little faces of the children, whose bodies I saw turned into wreaths of smoke beneath a silent blue sky. . . . Never shall I forget that nocturnal silence which deprived me, for all eternity, of the desire to live. Never shall I forget those moments which murdered my God and my soul and turned my dreams to dust. Never shall I forget these things, even if I am condemned to live as long as God Himself. Never.

Wiesel writes how on one train ride the prisoners received no food, had to live on snow, and daily new corpses would have to be thrown from the train. The Germans would sometimes throw a crust of bread into the midst of the prisoners to see them fight over it. One old man managed to get a bit, as he went to eat it he was savagely beaten by a younger man behind him. "Meir, my boy, don't you recognize me? I'm your father. . . you're hurting me. . . You're killing your father. I have some bread . . . for you too . . . for you too. . . ."

He collapsed and died, still clinging to the bread. His son searched him, took the bread, but before he could devour it other, stronger men fell on him. When these others withdrew, Wiesel writes, "next to me were two corpses, side by side, the father and the son. I was fifteen years old."

He writes of the SS publicly hanging a thirteen-year-old boy, with the face of a sad angel.

"Where is God? Where is He?" someone behind me asked. The guards marched all the prisoners past the gallows to force them to observe.

For more than half an hour he stayed there, struggling between life and death, dying in slow agony under our eyes. And we had to look him in the face. He was still alive when I passed in front of him. His tongue was still red, his eyes were not yet glazed.

Behind me, I heard the same man asking:

"Where is God now?"

And I heard a voice within me answer him:

"Where is He? Here He is — He is hanging here on this gallows."

Many years later Wiesel met a great French literary figure, François Mauriac. Mauriac told Wiesel that he must tell his story, must testify to the world the truth of what had happened. Wiesel asked Mauriac to write the preface to his first book, and these are Mauriac's concluding words about when Wiesel first met and posed this question — Where was God — to Mauriac while still a young man:

And I, who believe that God is love, what answer could I give my young questioner, whose dark eyes still held the reflection of that angelic sadness which had appeared one day upon the face of the hanged child? What did I say to him? Did I speak of that other Israeli, his brother, who may have resembled him — the Crucified, whose Cross has conquered the world? Did I affirm that the stumbling block to his faith was the cornerstone of mine, and that the conformity between the Cross and the suffering of men was in my eyes the key to that impenetrable mystery whereon the faith of his childhood had perished? . . . We do not know the worth of one single drop of blood, one single tear. All is grace. If the Eternal is the Eternal, the last word for each one of us belongs to Him. This is what I should have told this Jewish child. But I could only embrace him, weeping.

Where is God? Where is he in the midst of human raggedness and suffering and pain? Where is he in *your* pain, and mine? Though I marvel at the great stories of suffering and pain, I have my own. Small by comparison, but hard for me to understand. Where is God when the cancer comes, when love becomes betrayal, when the womb of one who longs to give life remains barren, when joy is strangled by guilt?

> Somehow it is in the cross that the glory of God is finally revealed.

"Where is he? He is here — he is here hanging on this gallows. . . ."

This is the central affirmation of the New Testament. Only it is not the *idea* of God that has died, as Nietzsche said. It was God *himself*. "We proclaim Christ crucified," Paul said.

It could have been worse. It could have happened to me. "Let it be so," God said. "Let it happen to me." And it did. All the wretchedness and misery of the human condition happened to God. "He became flesh and dwelt among us, and we beheld his glory." We saw the omnipotent One grow weary and fatigued. We saw the Creator of joy weep with sadness over death. We saw the One who spoke the Milky Way into being hammering nails and sawing planks to make benches and tables. We saw the Lord of Hosts spat upon and beaten up and bloodied. We saw Love himself betrayed and denied and doubted and abandoned by his closest friends. We saw the Righteous Judge become the unprotesting victim of history's greatest act of injustice. We saw Mary's little boy grow up to fulfill the prophecy given his mother at his birth: "And a sword will pierce your own soul too."

The pain and suffering and sin of this world leads only to the cross. Always the cross. And somehow it is in the cross that the glory of God is finally revealed.

"As soon as Judas had taken the bread, he went out. And it was night. When he was gone, Jesus said, 'Now is the Son of Man glorified and God is glorified in him.' "

As he prepares to go to the cross, Jesus prays, "Father, the time has come. Glorify your Son, that your Son may glorify you. . . And now, Father, glorify me in your presence with the glory I had with you before the world began."

"The Word became flesh and lived among us, and we have seen his glory, the glory as of a father's only son, full of grace and truth."

We have seen his glory, John says. That's just what people thought Jesus didn't have. Born in a manger, raised in obscurity, trained as carpenter, killed as criminal. A funny kind of glory. A strange way to save the world.

Martin Luther wrote that true knowledge of God will not lead to what he called a "theology of glory," but is rather based on a theology of the cross. Left to our own devices, Luther said, we would always think of God in terms of power and dominance and control. We would make him after our own image — we would think of him as *we* would want to be if we were God.

But this is not the God who reveals himself in Jesus. We see God most clearly when we see him in light of the cross. The cross is the foolishness of God that is wiser than human wisdom, the weakness of God that is stronger than human strength. Through the cross God reveals his humility and servanthood. In the cross we see God in all his raggedness.

For the glory of God is the raggedness of God. The most glorious aspect of his being is that he would take our raggedness upon himself before he would give us up. Karl Barth says that God would rather share in the suffering of human wretchedness than to be the blessed God of unblessed creatures.

God became like us — became one of us — and we beheld his glory.

GOD KNOCKING AT MY DOOR

I knew something of the upside and downside of glory. I grew up a Chicago Cubs fan in the late 1960s. Their entire infield made the all-star team one year. Randy Hundley, the catcher, was a personal favorite.

One day the phone rang. A neighbor, a girl in my class at school, got my mother on the phone.

"Mrs. Ortberg, you'll never guess what. Randy Hundley is at my house! I told him John lives next door. He wants to come to your house. Wants to see John."

Then something went terribly wrong.

My mother did not know who Randy Hundley was. Like the Pharaoh who "knew not Joseph," she had never heard of him. She thought he was some kid I went to school with, who wanted to come over and play. My mother said:

"Johnny is at piano lessons. You'll have to tell Randy he can come over and play some other day."

My mother was a pea-brain.

When I got home, my mother told me somebody named Randy Hundley had been next door, had wanted to come over, and she told him maybe some other time.

I wanted to call the social services people. Take my mother away.

That afternoon I was in a deep depression. Around 5:00 there was a knock on the door. When I answered it, there stood Randy Hundley. Major league baseball player. All-star. I beheld his glory — the glory of a professional catcher, full of power and a strong right arm.

He had stopped by our neighbors' before a speaking engagement, which is when my friend called. After he had finished speaking, although he was a major leaguer with a busy life, he decided to make a stop before he went home to Chicago.

He came all the way back to our neighborhood. He tracked down my house. He knocked on my door. "I didn't want you to take it out on your piano teacher," he said. He encouraged me to keep following Christ. He gave me an autographed baseball. (Which my mother seems to have thrown away, probably to make room for my sister's rag doll. At any rate, I can't find it.)

To a ten-year-old kid, the glory of Randy Hundley wasn't that he had a Howitzer for an arm. It wasn't that he caught Ferguson Jenkins and Kenny Holtzman, or that he hit long home runs off Bob Gibson and Nolan Ryan.

Glory was that someone as important as he was would take the time to come to the home of a little kid. *Glory* was that one day he laid aside his glove and bat and came knocking on my door. One day, he came just for me.

"The Word became flesh and lived among us, and we have seen his glory," John wrote. We beheld his glory when the Lord of all voluntarily submitted to his mother and father in all things. We beheld his glory when the Maker of heaven and earth used a saw and a hammer and nails to fashion chairs and benches. We beheld his glory when the Lord of hosts girded himself with a towel and carried a basin and washed the feet of his followers. We beheld his glory when the Author of life died on a cross. We beheld his glory when death could not hold him, the tomb could not imprison him.

We behold his glory still when he comes to ordinary, fallen human beings. For the glory of God is not just his power and might and majesty. His glory is that he would come to this corner of the universe, to this insignificant planet, to a ragged people he could not bring himself to discard. His glory is that one day he laid aside his majesty and bliss and came knocking at your door.

One day, he came just for you.

SOURCES

All italics in quotations have been added by the author and are not in the original unless otherwise noted. Scripture quotations are from the *New Revised Standard Version* unless otherwise indicated.

Chapter 1: *Love Beyond Reason*

11: *Augustine:* Cited in M. C. D'Arcy, *The Mind and Heart of Love*. New York: Henry Holt, 1947, 87.

15: *Thorp:* Karen Lee-Thorp, *Why Beauty Matters*. Colorado Springs: NavPress, 1997.

16: *Lewis:* C. S. Lewis, *The Four Loves*. Glasgow: William Collins, 1960, 116

16: *"While we were still weak":* Romans 5:6 – 8.

16: *"All of us have become":* Isaiah 64:6 NIV.

17: *Lewis:* Lewis, *The Four Loves*, 121.

20: *"That you may become blameless":* Philippians 2:15 NIV.

21: *Allender:* Dan B. Allender and Tremper Longman III, *Bold Love*. Colorado Springs: NavPress, 1992, back cover.

21: *"For the Lord disciplines":* Hebrews 12:6.

21: *"To present the church":* Ephesians 5:27.

21: *"And sent his Son":* 1 John 4:10.

22: *"If God is for us":* Romans 8:31, 35.

22: *"Even now he is coming":* Exodus 4:14.

23: *"As the apple of the eye":* Psalm 17:8.

23: *"You are the apple":* See Lloyd Ogilvie, *Falling into Greatness*. Nashville: Thomas Nelson, 1984, 45.

23: *"When Israel was a child":* Hosea 11:1 – 4, 7.

24: *Williams:* Charles Williams, *He Came Down from Heaven*. Grand Rapids: Eerdmans, 1984, 107.

24: *"God so loved the world":* John 3:16.

28: *"See what love the Father":* 1 John 3:1 – 2.

Chapter 2: *Love Pays Attention*

29: *Owens:* Virginia Stem Owens, *And the Trees Clap Their Hands.* Grand Rapids: Eerdmans, 1983.

30: *Erikson:* Erik H. Erikson, *Insight and Responsibility.* New York: W. W. Norton, 1964, 102.

30: *Egan:* Gerald Egan, *The Skilled Helper.* Belmont, CA: Wadsworth, 1975, 62.

31: *"The LORD bless you":* Numbers 6:24 – 26 NIV.

31: *" 'Come,' my heart says":* Psalm 27:8 – 9.

32: *"If I were a rich man":* From the musical *Fiddler on the Roof,* music by Jerry Bock, lyrics by Sheldon Harnick, based on stories by Sholem Aleichem.

32: *"As he walked along":* John 9:1.

34: *"O LORD, you have searched me":* Psalm 139:1.

34: *"Are not two sparrows sold":* Matthew 10:29 – 30.

34: *"Who sinned, this man":* John 9:2.

35: *Ellison:* Ralph Ellison, *The Invisible Man.* New York: Random House, 1963.

37: *"Remember that you were":* Deuteronomy 5:15.

37: *"The neighbors and those":* John 9:8 – 9.

38: *"We know that this is our son":* John 9:20 – 21.

38: *Newbigin:* Lesslie Newbigin, *The Light Has Come.* Grand Rapids: Eerdmans, 1982, 122.

39: *"I told you once":* John 9:27 ANCHOR BIBLE.

39: *"Listen, you that are deaf":* Isaiah 42:18 – 20.

39: *Barry:* William Barry and William Connolly, *The Practice of Spiritual Direction.* San Francisco: HarperCollins, 1993, 33.

41: *"Be still, and know":* Psalm 46:10.

41: *"O LORD, my heart is not":* Psalm 131:1 – 2.

44: *Tannen:* Deborah Tannen, *You Just Don't Understand.* New York: Morrow, 1990, 113 – 14.

44: *"Let everyone be quick":* James 1:19.

45: *Peck:* Scott Peck, *The Road Less Traveled.* New York: Simon & Schuster, 1978, 120.

Chapter 3: *God Touches the Untouchable*

48: *Lewis:* C. S. Lewis, *The Four Loves.* Glasgow: William Collins, 1960, 111.

49: *Smalley:* Gary Smalley and John Trent, *The Blessing.* Nashville: Thomas Nelson, 1986, 41 – 42.

49: *The Economist:* 8 October 1994, 17.

49: *Brand:* Paul Brand, *Pain: The Gift Nobody Wants.* New York: Harper Collins, 1993.

50: *"The person who has":* Leviticus 13:45 – 46.

50: William Barclay *The Gospel of Mark.* The Daily Study Bible. Philadelphia: Westminster Press, 1963.

50: *"If you choose":* Mark 1:40.

51: *"If you are able":* Mark 9:22.

54: *"In order that he might":* Mark 10:13.

55: *"Moved with pity":* Mark 1:41.

57: *Lewis:* Lewis, *The Four Loves,* 111 – 12.

Chapter 4: *The Lord of the Second Chance*

61: *Smedes:* Lewis B. Smedes, *Forgive and Forget.* San Francisco: Harper & Row, 1984, 11.

63: *Frazier:* Charles Frazier, *Cold Mountain.* New York: Atlantic Monthly Press, 1997, 30.

64: *"Children, you haven't caught":* Paraphrase of John 21:5.

65: *"Put your boat in deep water":* Paraphrase of Luke 5:4.

65: *"Go away from me":* Luke 5:8.

67: *Harris:* Murray Harris, unpublished chapel talk at Trinity Evangelical Divinity School.

67: *"Do you love me?":* From the musical *Fiddler on the Roof,* music by Jerry Bock, lyrics by Sheldon Harnick, based on stories by Sholem Aleichem.

68: *Stylistic variation:* See Raymond Brown, *The Gospel of John, Vol. 1,* in the Anchor Bible. Garden City, NY: Doubleday, 1966, 370.

71: *"As a father has compassion":* Psalm 103:13.

72: *Bennis:* Warren Bennis and Burt Nanus, *Leaders.* New York: Harper & Row, 1985, 76.

74: *"His love has no limits":* Annie Johnson Flint.

Chapter 5: *Jesus the Teacher*

75: *Smith:* C. W. F. Smith, *The Jesus of the Parables*. Philadelphia: Westminster Press, 1948, 19.

78: *Buechner:* Frederick Buechner, *Telling the Truth*. San Francisco: Harper & Row, 1977, 62 – 63.

80: *Palmer:* Earl Palmer, *Laughter in Heaven*. Waco, TX: Word Books, 1980, 79ff.

81: *"There are various kinds":* 1 Corinthians 3:12 – 15 LIVING BIBLE.

81: *Fromm:* Erich Fromm, *Escape from Freedom*.

82: *Tournier:* Paul Tournier, *The Meaning of Persons*. New York: Harper & Row, 1973, 205.

83: *"The rain came down":* Matthew 7:27 NIV.

85: *"Don't worry about tomorrow":* Matthew 6:34 paraphrased.

87: *Plantinga:* Cornelius Plantinga, *Not the Way It's Supposed to Be*. Grand Rapids: Eerdmans, 1995, 121.

88: *Keillor:* Garrison Keillor, *Lake Wobegon Days*. New York: Penguin Books, 1985, 413 – 14.

Chapter 6: *The Contentment of Being Loved*

91: *Buechner:* Frederick Buechner, *The Longing for Home: Recollections and Reflections*. New York: Harper Collins, 1996, 129.

94: *Frankl:* Viktor Frankl, *Man's Search for Meaning*. New York: Washington Square Press, 1963, xiii.

94: *"Vanity of vanities":* Ecclesiastes 1:2, 8.

94: *Mouw:* Richard Mouw, personal conversation.

95: *"For the creation was subjected":* Romans 8:20 – 21.

96: *"When they came to Marah":* Exodus 15:23 – 24.

96: *"The whole congregation":* Exodus 16:2 – 3.

97: *"The rabble among them":* Numbers 11:4 – 6.

98: *"Why have you treated":* Numbers 11:11 – 15.

98: *"Consecrate yourselves":* Numbers 11:18.

98: *"You shall eat not only":* Numbers 11:19 – 20.

99: *"Hope and a future":* See Jeremiah 29:11 NIV.

99: *Hughes:* Robert Hughes, *The Culture of Complaint: The Fraying of America*. New York: Oxford University Press, 1993.

100: *Cheever:* John Cheever. Source unknown.

100: *Warren:* Neil Clark Warren, *Finding Contentment.* Nashville: Thomas Nelson, 1997, 26.

100: *"Ho, everyone who thirsts":* Isaiah 55:1 – 2.

102: *Barrie:* See story by J. M. Barrie in *The Little, Brown Book of Anecdotes,* ed. Clifton Fadiman. Boston: Little, Brown, 1985, 39 – 40.

103: *"Weariness of the flesh":* Ecclesiastes 12:12.

103: *Foster:* Richard Foster, *Prayer.* San Francisco: Harper Collins, 1992, introduction, 3 – 4.

105: *Smedes:* Lewis B. Smedes. Source unknown.

105: *Recipe:* From Cornelius Plantinga, *Not the Way It's Supposed to Be.* Grand Rapids: Eerdmans, 1995, 14.

106: *"Let me live that I may":* Psalm 119:175.

106: *Chesterton:* G. K. Chesterton. Source unknown.

Chapter 7: The Roundabout Way

111. *Merton:* Thomas Merton, *New Seeds of Contemplation.* New York: New Directions, 1972, 239.

112: *"Bring them up":* Exodus 3:8.

112: *"When Pharaoh let the people":* Exodus 13:17 – 18.

113: *Mouw:* Richard Mouw, *Uncommon Decency.* Grand Rapids: Eerdmans, 1995.

114: *Old Testament scholars:* See *The Interpreter's Dictionary of the Bible,* vol. 3. Nashville: Abingdon, 1985, 565.

117: *Lewis:* C. S. Lewis, *The Screwtape Letters.* New York: Macmillan, 1975, 47.

118: *"They may change their minds":* Exodus 13:17.

118: *Joseph:* See Genesis 37; 39 – 41; 50:22 – 26; Exodus 13:19.

118: *David:* See 1 Samuel 16; 18 – 19; 22 – 24.

118: *Daniel:* See Daniel 1; 6.

122: *Childs:* Brevard Childs, *The Book of Exodus: A Critical, Theological Commentary.* Old Testament Library. Louisville: Westminster John Knox, 1974.

122: *Buechner:* Frederick Buechner, *A Room Called Remember.* New York: Harper & Row, 1984: quoted in Bob Benson Sr. and Michael W. Benson, *Disciplines of the Inner Life.* Nashville: Thomas Nelson, 1989, 85.

125: *MacLean:* Norman MacLean, *Young Men and Fire.* Chicago: University of Chicago Press, 1992, 38.

126: *MacLean:* MacLean, *Young Men and Fire,* 299: quoting Matthew 27:46.

Chapter 8: *Love and Grace*

128: *Luther:* Martin Luther, "A Sermon on the Eve of the Sunday Before Reminiscere," *Selected Writings of Martin Luther,* ed. Theodore Tappert. Philadelphia: Fortress Press, 1967, 259.

128: *Campolo:* Adapted from Tony Campolo, *The Kingdom of God Is a Party.* Dallas: Word Books, 1990, 6 – 9.

130: *Yancey:* Philip Yancey, *What's So Amazing About Grace?* Grand Rapids: Zondervan, 1997, 15.

131: *Van Auken:* Sheldon Van Auken, *A Severe Mercy.* San Francisco: Harper & Row, 1977, 85.

131: *Willard:* Dallas Willard, *The Spirit of the Disciplines.* San Francisco: Harper Collins, 1989, 80 – 81.

134: *"Love the Lord your God":* Luke 10:27.

134: *"And if I have prophetic powers":* 1 Corinthians 13:2.

134: *"Whoever does not love":* 1 John 4:8.

137: *"Circumcised on the eighth day":* Philippians 3:5 – 6.

138: *Series of metaphors:* See Colossians 2:11 – 15.

140: *"Who will separate us"* See Romans 8:35 – 39.

141: *"My grace is sufficient":* 2 Corinthians 12:9.

141: *"God opposes the proud":* 1 Peter 5:5.

142: *"Certain intruders":* Jude 4.

142: *Prodigal son:* See Luke 15:11 – 32.

143: *Craddock:* Fred Craddock: quoted in Yancey, *What's So Amazing About Grace?*

144: *Bonhoeffer:* Dietrich Bonhoeffer, *The Cost of Discipleship.* New York: Macmillan, 1976, 60.

146: *"The Word became flesh":* John 1:14.

146: *"We played the flute":* Matthew 11:17; Luke 7:32.

Chapter 9: *Being Loved Means Being Chosen*

148: *Thomas:* Thomas à Kempis, *The Imitation of Christ.* Reprint, Nashville: Thomas Nelson, 1976, 98.

149: *The Whisper Test*: Quoted in Les Parrott, *High-Maintenance Relationships*. Wheaton, IL: Tyndale House, 1996, 206.

150: *Roberts*: Robert Roberts, *Taking the Word to Heart*. Grand Rapids: Eerdmans, 1993, 156.

152: *"I now realize how true"*: Acts 10:34 NIV.

152: *Lasch*: Christopher Lasch, *The Culture of Narcissism*. New York: W. W. Norton, 1978, xv.

153: *"Rabbi, the one who was"*: John 3:26.

156: *Fiddler on the Roof*: Music by Jerry Bock, lyrics by Sheldon Harnick, based on stories by Sholem Aleichem.

157: *Boris*: Harold Boris, *Envy*. Northvale, NJ: Jason Aronson, 1994, xv.

157: *"Rejoice with those who rejoice"*: Romans 12:15 NIV.

157: *Rogers*: Samuel Rogers: quoted in Clifton Fadiman, *The Little, Brown Book of Anecdotes*. Boston: Little, Brown, 1985, 474.

158: *Buechner*: Frederick Buechner, *Peculiar Treasures*. New York: Harper & Row, 1973, 20.

158: *Cain and Abel*: See Genesis 4:1 – 16.

159: *Boris*: Boris, *Envy*, 155.

160: *"Saul has killed"*: 1 Samuel 21:11.

160: *"They have ascribed to David"*: 1 Samuel 18:8 – 9.

160: *Plantinga*: Cornelius Plantinga, *Not the Way It's Supposed to Be: A Breviary of Sin*. Grand Rapids: Eerdmans, 1995, 156ff.

161: *Siblings Without Rivalry*: Adele Faber and Elaine Mazlish, *Siblings Without Rivalry*. New York: W. W. Norton, 1987, 88.

161: *"As God's chosen ones"*: Colossians 3:12.

162: *Faber*: Faber and Mazlish, *Siblings Without Rivalry*, 89.

162: *"No one can receive anything"*: John 3:27.

163: *"Prepare the way of the Lord"*: Matthew 3:3.

165: *"He must become greater"*: John 3:30.

165: *"He must increase"*: John 3:30 KJV.

Chapter 10: *Safe in God's Love*

166: *Willard*: Dallas Willard, *The Divine Conspiracy*. San Francisco: Harper Collins, 1998, 66, italics in original.

167: *Elisha and the Arameans*: 2 Kings 6:8 – 23; some quotations paraphrased.

169: *Willard:* Dallas Willard, *The Divine Conspiracy.* San Francisco: Harper Collins, 1998, 66.

169: *"Who will separate us":* Romans 8:35.

169: *"Yea, though I walk":* Psalm 23:4 KJV.

170: *"Without warning, a furious storm":* Matthew 8:23 NIV.

171: *Berkeley psychology student:* See Gilbert Brim, *Ambition.* San Francisco: Basic Books, 1992, 9 – 10.

173: *Time:* Date of issue unknown.

173: *"He was deeply moved":* John 11:33 NIV.

173: *"I tell you the truth":* John 13:21 NIV.

173: *"Besides everything else":* 2 Corinthians 11:28 – 29 NIV.

174: *"Let the word of Christ":* Colossians 3:16.

174: *"Why do you worry":* Matthew 6:25 paraphrased.

175: *"Peace I leave with you":* John 14:27.

176: *"About midnight Paul and Silas":* Acts 16:25.

176: *"But I trust in your":* Psalm 13:5 – 6 NIV.

176: *"You turned my wailing":* Psalm 30:11 – 12 NIV.

176: *"Sing psalms, hymns":* Ephesians 5:19 paraphrased.

177: *"Cast all your anxiety":* 1 Peter 5:7.

177: *Swenson:* Richard Swenson, in a public address.

178: *"Do not be anxious":* Philippians 4:6 NIV.

180: *"See what love the Father":* 1 John 3:1.

180: *Luther:* Martin Luther: quoted in Roland Bainton, *Here I Stand.* Nashville: Abingdon, 1950, 173.

182: *"I have called you by my name":* Isaiah 43:1 – 4.

Chapter 11: *God Searches for Hiding People*

184: *Caussade:* Jean Pierre de Caussade, *The Sacrament of the Present Moment.* San Francisco: Harper Collins, 1989, 18 – 19.

184: *Chesterton:* G. K. Chesterton, *Tremendous Trifles.* New York: Dodd, Mead, 1901, 56.

184: *Fulghum:* See Robert Fulghum, *All I Really Need to Know I Learned in Kindergarten.* New York: Villard Books, 1987, 56 – 58.

185: *"They heard the sound":* Genesis 3:8 – 10.

187: *"You will seek me":* Jeremiah 29:13 NIV.

187: *Thompson:* Francis Thompson, "The Hound of Heaven." 1893.

187: *"They were naked":* Genesis 2:25 paraphrased.

188: *"Adam, where are you":* See Genesis 3:9.

189: *"All we like sheep":* Isaiah 53:6.

190: *The story of the lost sheep:* See Luke 15:3 – 7.

191: *Keller:* Phillip Keller, *A Shepherd Looks at the 23rd Psalm.* Grand Rapids: Zondervan, 1996, 51 – 52.

193: *Zacchaeus:* See Luke 19:1 – 9.

194: *"The best among physicians":* Jeremias Joachim, *Jerusalem in the Time of Jesus.* Philadelphia: Fortress Press, 1989, 303ff.

196: *Levi/Matthew:* See Luke 5:27 – 32.

197: *Time:* Date of issue unknown.

Chapter 12: *The Ragged God*

200: *"The Word became flesh":* John 1:14.

200: *Wiesel:* Elie Wiesel, *All Rivers Run to the Sea.* New York: Alfred A. Knopf, 1995, 85.

200: *Kierkegaard:* Søren Kierkegaard, *Philosophical Fragments.* Princeton, NJ: Princeton University Press, 1974, 34 – 35.

202: *Kierkegaard:* Kierkegaard, *Philosophical Fragments,* 40.

202: *"And this shall be a sign":* Luke 2:12 KJV.

202: *"Foxes have holes":* Luke 9:58.

202: *"He had no form":* Isaiah 53:2.

202: *"No one has seen God":* John 1:18.

203: *Lewis:* C. S. Lewis, *The Screwtape Letters.* New York: Macmillan, 1975, letter 4.

203: *New York:* Quoted in Cornelius Plantinga, *Not the Way It's Supposed to Be.* Grand Rapids: Eerdmans, 1995, 84.

204: *Wiesel:* Wiesel, *All Rivers Run to the Sea,* 164.

204: *"Show me your glory":* Exodus 33:18.

205: *"I will make all my goodness":* Exodus 33:19.

205: *Wiesel:* Elie Wiesel, *Night.* New York: Hill and Wang, 1987, 43.

206: *Wiesel:* Wiesel, *Night,* 71 – 72.

207: *Mauriac:* Wiesel, *Night,* 11.

208: *"We proclaim Christ":* 1 Corinthians 1:23.

208: *"He became flesh":* John 1:14 paraphrased.

208: *"And a sword will pierce":* Luke 2:35.

209: *"As soon as Judas":* John 13:30 – 31 NIV.

209: *"Father, the time has come":* John 17: 1, 5 NIV.

209: *Luther:* Martin Luther: see Philip Watson, *Let God Be God.* Philadelphia: Fortress Press, 1970, 78.

WHEN THE GAME

IS OVER

IT ALL GOES

BACK IN THE BOX

JOHN ORTBERG

BESTSELLING AUTHOR

CHAPTER ONE

LEARN RULE 1

This is our predicament.
Over and over again,
we lose sight of what is important and what isn't.
EPICTETUS[1]

My grandmother had just gotten out of jail.

She was a roll away from the yellow properties. And the yellow properties meant trouble. They were mine. And they had hotels. And Gram had no money. She had wanted to stay in jail longer to avoid landing on my property and having to cough up dough she did not have, but she rolled doubles, and that meant her bacon was going to get fried.

I was a ten-year-old sitting at the Monopoly table. I had it all—money and property, houses and hotels, Boardwalk and Park Place. I had been a loser at this game my whole life, but today was different, as I knew it would be. Today I was Donald Trump, Bill Gates, Ivan the Terrible. Today my grandmother was one roll of the dice away from ruin. And I was one roll of the dice away from the biggest lesson life has to teach: the absolute necessity of arranging our life around what matters in light of our mortality and eternity. It is a lesson that some of the smartest people in the world forget but that my grandmother was laser clear on.

For my grandmother taught me how to play the game....

Golda Hall, my mother's mother, lived with us in the corner bedroom when I was growing up. She was a greathearted person. She was built soft and round, the way grandmothers were before they took up aerobics. She remains, at least in the memories of my boyhood, the most purely fun person I have known. She let us stay up later than we were supposed to on Friday nights when our parents were gone. She peeled apples for us, told us ghost stories and scary old poems ("Little Orphan Annie came to our house to stay ...") that kept us awake for hours. She baked banana bread that was like having dessert for breakfast and made us red velvet cake—which consists mostly of butter—on our birthdays.

And she taught me how to play the game.

My grandmother was a game player, and she did not like to lose. She didn't get mean or mad, but she still (to use an expression from her childhood world) had some snap in her girdle. It was part of her charm. Every Friday night as long as my grandfather was alive, the whole family, including spouses, would gather to play a card game called Rook; and if you were Gram's partner, it was not wise to miss a trick or lose the bid. Everyone's favorite old home movie featured Gram playing in a softball game at a family picnic in her younger days. She made contact with the ball and ran the bases with such singleness of purpose—a large woman coming at you like Bronco Nagurski—that no one got in her way. Home run. When she played Chinese checkers with small grandchildren, she was not one of those pushover grandmothers who would lose on purpose to make the grandchildren feel better about themselves. Gram believed before Max De Pree ever said it that a leader's first task is to define reality. She was the leader, and the reality was that she played to win. Pouting and self-pity, two of my spiritual gifts, did not elicit sympathy from her, for even when she was playing, she kept an eye on what kind of person you were becoming. And my grandmother taught me how to play the game.

THE MASTER OF THE BOARD

Grandmother was at her feistiest when it came to Monopoly. Periodically leaders like General Patton or Attila the Hun develop a reputation for toughness. They were lapdogs next to her. Imagine that Vince Lombardi had produced an offspring with Lady MacBeth, and you get some idea of the competitive streak that ran in my grandmother. She was a gentle and kind soul, but at the Monopoly table she would still take you to the cleaners.

When I got the initial $1,500 from the banker to start the game, I always wanted to hang on to my money as long as possible. You never know what Chance card might turn up next. The board is a risky place. I am half Swedish (on my father's side), and Swedes are not high rollers.

But my grandmother knew how to play the game. She understood that you don't win without risk, and she didn't play for second place. So she would spend every dollar she got. She would buy every piece of property she landed on. She would mortgage every piece of property she owned to the hilt in order to buy everything else.

She understood what I did not—that accumulating is the name of the game, that money is how you keep score, that the race goes to the swift. She played with skill, passion, and reckless abandon. Eventually, inevitably, she would become Master of the Board. When you're the Master of the Board, you own so much property that no one else can hurt you. When you're Master of the Board, you're in control. Other players regard you with fear and envy, shock and awe. From that point on, it's only a matter of time. She would watch me land on Boardwalk one time too many, hand over to her what was left of my money, and put my little race car marker away, all the time wondering why I had lost yet again. "Don't worry about it," she'd say. "One day you'll learn to play the game."

I hated it when she said that.

Then one year when I was ten, I spent a summer playing Monopoly every day with a kid named Steve who lived kitty-corner from me. Gradually it dawned on me that the only way to win this game was to make a total commitment to acquisition. No mercy. No fear. What my grandmother had been showing me for so long finally sank in.

By the fall, when we sat down to play, I was more ruthless than she was. My palms were sweaty. I would play without softness or caution. I was ready to bend the rules if I had to. Slowly, cunningly, I exposed the soft underbelly of my grandmother's vulnerability. Relentlessly, inexorably, I drove her off the board. (The game does strange things to you.)

I can still remember—it happened at Marvin Gardens.

I looked at my grandmother—this was the woman who had taught me how to play. She was an old lady by now. A widow. She had raised my mother. She loved my mother, as she loved me. And I took everything she had. I destroyed her financially and psychologically. I watched her give up her last dollar and quit in utter defeat.

It was the greatest moment of my life.

I had won. I was cleverer, and stronger, and more ruthless than anyone at the table. I was Master of the Board.

But then my grandmother had one more thing to teach me. The greatest lesson comes at the end of the game. And here it is. In the words of James Dobson, who described this lesson from Monopoly in playing with his family many years ago: *"Now it all goes back in the box."*

All those houses and hotels. All that property—Boardwalk and Park Place, the railroads and the utility companies. All those thousands of dollars. *When the game is over, it all goes back in the box.*

I didn't want it to go back in the box. I wanted to leave it out as a perpetual memorial to my skill at playing the game—to bronze it, perhaps, so others could admire my tenacity and success. I wanted the sense of power that goes with being Master of the Board to last forever. I wanted the thrill of winning to be my perpetual companion. I was so heady with victory after all these years that for a few moments I lost touch with reality. None of that stuff was mine—not really. Now, for a few moments, it was my turn to play the game. I could get all steamed up about it for a while and act as if the game were going to last forever. But it would not. Not for me. Not for you either. Plato said that the entire task of philosophy can be summed up as *melete thanatou*—"mindfulness of death."[2]

I am a Christian, and I seek to write this book from the perspective of faith. I believe that you are a ceaseless being with an eternal destiny in the universe of an unimaginably good God. But you don't even have to believe in the Bible to understand the lesson of the box. Comedian Jerry Seinfeld put it like this:

To me, if life boils down to one significant thing, it's movement. To live is to keep moving. Unfortunately, this means that for the rest of our lives we're going to be looking for boxes.

When you're moving, your whole world is boxes. That's all you think about. "Boxes, where are the boxes?" You just wander down the street going in and out of stores, "Are there boxes here? Have you seen any boxes?" It's all you think about.

You could be at a funeral, everyone around you is mourning, crying, and you're looking at the casket. "That's a nice box. Does anybody know where that guy got that box? When he's done with it, you think I could get it? It's got some nice handles on it. My stereo would fit right in there."

I mean that's what death is, really — the last big move of your life. The hearse is like the van, the pall bearers are your close friends, the only ones you could really ask to help you with a big move like that. And the casket is that great, perfect box you've been looking for your whole life.[3]

WHAT REALLY MATTERS?

It's not bad to play the game. It's not bad to be really good at it. It's not bad to be Master of the Board. My grandmother taught me to play to win. But there are always more rungs to climb, more money to be made, more deals to pull off. And the danger is that we forget to ask what really matters. We race around the board with shallow relationships, frenzied schedules, preoccupied souls. Being smart or strong does not protect you from this fate. In some ways, it makes the game more dangerous, for the temporary rewards you get from playing can lull you into pretending that the game will never end.

As a student in school, I may think that the game is won by getting better grades or making first string or getting elected class president. Then comes graduation and the pressure to win at my job, to get promoted, to have enough money to feel safe, and to be able to think of myself as successful. I pass somebody up and feel pleasure.

Someone passes me, and I feel a stab of pain. Always I hear this inner voice: *Is it enough? Did I do good?* And sometimes if I'm quiet: *Does it mean anything?*

Then the chase is for financial security, a well-planned retirement in an active senior community where Botox and Grecian Formula 44 and ginko biloba and Lipitor and Viagra bring chemically induced temporary immortality.

Then one day it stops. Other people keep going. Somewhere on the board, somebody is just getting started. But for you, the game is over. Did you play wisely? We all want God, Anne Lamott writes, but left to our own devices, we seek all the worldly things — possessions, money, looks, and power — because we think they will bring us fulfillment. "But this turns out to be a joke, because they are just props, and when we check out of this life, we have to give them all back to the great prop master in the sky. They're just on loan. They're not ours."[4] They all go back in the box.

LIVE DIFFERENTLY—STARTING NOW

Human beings are the only creatures whose frontal lobes are so developed that they know that the game will end. This is our glory, our curse, our warning, and our opportunity. In Jerusalem, hundreds of synagogues have been built by Jews from around the world. One was built by a group from Budapest, and according to an ancient custom, they had a coffin built into the wall. There is no body in it, they explain to visitors; it is present as a silent witness to remind us that it all goes back in the box.

The Talmud teaches that every person should fully repent one day before his death. When a visitor asked, "But how will I know when that day is?" he was told: "Treat every day as if it were the day before your last."[5] Arrange your life around what matters most. Starting today. The box will wait.

This is how my grandmother taught me to play the game of my life, and I talk about that in the pages that follow. My grandmother led, in many ways, a pretty simple life. She never went to high school, never led a company, never wrote a book, never traveled the world.

She met her lifelong sweetheart in the eighth grade, her last year of formal education. She gave birth to three sons named — I'm not making this up — Hack, Jack, and Mac (the names Huey, Dewey, and Louie already having been taken by Donald Duck's nephews), and then three girls, including my mother. She never moved outside the state where she was born. The only paid job she ever had that I know of was working behind the counter in a little Swedish bakery.

She was content with her life because she believed she knew what mattered. She had a clear understanding about what she thought was temporal and what was eternal. Everybody has to decide what he or she believes counts as winning and losing in life. One of the smartest men who ever lived told one of his most unforgettable stories about exactly that decision. That's for the next chapter. But I've had a long time to think about it.

My grandmother taught me how to play the game.

ENDNOTES: LEARN RULE 1

1. Epictetus, *The Art of Living: The Classic Manual on Virtue, Happiness, and Effectiveness.* A new interpretation by Sharon Lebell. New York: HarperCollins, 1994, 105.

2. Daniel Goleman, *Vital Lies, Simple Truths.* New York: Simon & Schuster, 1985, 237.

3. *Seinfeld* (television program): www.seinfeldscripts.com/TheBoyfriend2. htm.

4. Anne Lamott, *Bird by Bird: Some Instructions on Writing and Life.* New York: Doubleday, 1994, 195.

5. Benjamin Blech, *The Complete Idiot's Guide to Understanding Judaism.* New York: Alpha Books, 1999, 157.

WILLOW CREEK ASSOCIATION

This resource is just one of many ministry tools published in partnership with the Willow Creek Association. Founded in 1992, WCA was created to serve churches and church leaders striving to create environments where those still outside the family of God are welcomed—and can more easily consider God's loving offer of salvation through faith.

These innovative churches and leaders are connected at the deepest level by their all-out dedication to Christ and His Kingdom. Willing to do whatever it required to build churches that help people move along the path toward Christ-centered devotion; they also share a deep desire to encourage all believers at every step of their faith journey, to continue moving toward a fully transformed, Christ-centered life.

Today, more than 10,000 churches from 80 denominations worldwide are formally connected to WCA and each other through WCA Membership. Many thousands more come to WCA for networking, training, and resources.

For more information about the ministry of the
Willow Creek Association, visit: **willowcreek.com**.

Soul Keeping

Caring for the Most Important Part of You

Bestselling Author John Ortberg

The soul is NOT "a theological and abstract subject."

The soul is the coolest, eeriest, most mysterious, evocative, crucial, sacred, eternal, life-directing, fragile, indestructible, controversial, expensive dimension of your existence.

Jesus said it's worth more than the world.

You'd be an idiot not to prize it above all else.

Shouldn't you get pretty clear on exactly what it is? Shouldn't you know what it runs on? Wouldn't it be worth knowing how to care for it?

Two things are for sure. One is: you have a soul. The other is: if you don't look after this one, you won't be issued a replacement.

Bestselling author John Ortberg writes another classic that will help readers discover their soul and take their relationship with God to the next level.

Available in stores and online!

ZONDERVAN®
.com

Who Is This Man?

The Unpredictable Impact of the Inescapable Jesus

Bestselling Author John Ortberg

Jesus' impact on our world is highly unlikely, widely inescapable, largely unknown, and decidedly double-edged. It is unlikely in light of the severe limitations of his earthly life; it is inescapable because of the range of impact; it is unknown because history doesn't connect dots; and it is doubled-edged because his followers have wreaked so much havoc, often in his name.

He is history's most familiar figure, yet he is the man no one knows. His impact on the world is immense and non-accidental. From the Dark Ages to post-modernity, he is the Man who won't go away.

And yet ... you can miss him in historical lists for many reasons, maybe the most obvious being the way he lived his life. He did not loudly and demonstrably defend his movement in the spirit of a rising political or military leader. He did not lay out a case that history would judge his brand of belief superior in all future books.

His life and teaching simply drew people to follow him. He made history by starting in a humble place, in a spirit of love and acceptance, and allowing each person space to respond.

His vision of life continues to haunt and challenge humanity. His influence has swept over history bringing inspiration to what has happened in art, science, government, medicine, and education; he has taught humans about dignity, compassion, forgiveness, and hope.

Five-Session DVD Study also available.

Available in stores and online!

ZONDERVAN
.com

The Life You've Always Wanted

Spiritual Disciplines for Ordinary People

Bestselling Author John Ortberg

You can live a deeper, more spiritual life right where you are.

The heart of Christianity is transformation—a relationship with God that impacts not just our spiritual lives but every aspect of our daily lives. John Ortberg calls readers back to the dynamic heartbeat of Christianity—God's power to bring change and growth—and reveals how and why transformation takes place.

The Life You've Always Wanted offers modern perspectives on the ancient path of the spiritual disciplines. But it is more than just a book about things to do to be a good Christian. It's a road map toward true transformation that starts not with the individual but with the person at the journey's end—Jesus Christ.

As with a marathon runner, the secret to finishing a race lies not in trying harder, but in training consistently—training with the spiritual disciplines. The disciplines are neither taskmasters nor ends in themselves. Rather they are exercises that build strength and endurance for the road of growth. The fruit of the Spirit—joy, peace, kindness, etc.—are the signposts along the way.

Paved with humor and sparkling anecdotes, *The Life You've Always Wanted* is an encouraging and challenging approach to a Christian life that's worth living—a life on the edge that fills an ordinary world with new meaning, hope, change, and joy.

Available in stores and online!

ZONDERVAN®
.com

When the Game Is Over, It All Goes Back in the Box

Bestselling Author John Ortberg

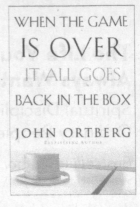

Remember the thrill of winning at checkers or Parcheesi? You become the Master of the Board — the victor over everyone else. But what happens after that? asks bestselling author John Ortberg. You know the answer: It all goes back in the box. You don't get to keep one token, one chip, one game card. In the end, the spoils of the game add up to nothing.

Using popular games as a metaphor for our temporal lives, *When the Game Is Over, It All Goes Back in the Box* neatly sorts out what's fleeting and what's permanent in God's kingdom. Being Master of the Board is not the point; being rich toward God is. Winning the game of life on Earth is a temporary victory; loving God and other people with all our hearts is an eternal one. Using humor, terrific stories, and a focus on winning "the right trophies," Ortberg paints a vivid picture of the priorities that all Christians will want to embrace.

When the Game Is Over, It All Goes Back in the Box

Six Sessions on Living Life in the Light of Eternity

John Ortberg with Stephen and Amanda Sorenson

In the six sessions you will learn how to:
- Live passionately and boldly
- Learn how to be active players in the game that pleases God
- Find your true mission and offer your best
- Fill each square on the board with what matters most
- Seek the richness of being instead of the richness of having

If You Want to Walk on Water, You've Got to Get Out of the Boat

Bestselling Author John Ortberg

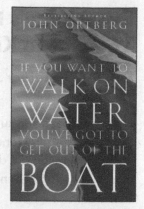

Deep within you lies the same faith and longing that sent Peter walking across the wind-swept Sea of Galilee toward Jesus.

John Ortberg invites you to consider the incredible potential that awaits you outside your comfort zone. Out on the risky waters of faith, Jesus is waiting to meet you in ways that will change you forever, deepening your character and your trust in God. The experience is terrifying. It's thrilling beyond belief. It's everything you'd expect of someone worthy to be called Lord.

The choice is yours to know him as only a water-walker can, aligning yourself with God's purpose for your life in the process. There's just one requirement: *If You Want to Walk on Water, You've Got to Get Out of the Boat.*

Six-Session DVD Study also available.

Available in stores and online!

Everybody's Normal Till You Get to Know Them

Bestselling Author John Ortberg

Not you, that's for sure! No one you've ever met, either. None of us are normal according to God's definition, and the closer we get to each other, the plainer that becomes.

Yet for all our quirks, sins, and jagged edges, we need each other. Community is more than just a word —it is one of our most fundamental requirements. So how do flawed, abnormal people such as ourselves master the forces that can drive us apart and come together in the life-changing relationships God designed us for?

In *Everybody's Normal Till You Get to Know Them*, teacher and bestselling author John Ortberg zooms in on the things that make community tick. You'll get a thought-provoking look at God's heart, at others, and at yourself. Even better, you'll gain wisdom and tools for drawing closer to others in powerful, impactful ways. With humor, insight, and a gift for storytelling, Ortberg shows how community pays tremendous dividends in happiness, health, support, and growth. It's where all of us weird, unwieldy people encounter God's love in tangible ways and discover the transforming power of being loved, accepted, and valued just the way we are.

Available in stores and online!

ZONDERVAN®
.com

God Is Closer
Than You Think

This Can Be the Greatest Moment of Your Life Because This Moment Is the Place Where You Can Meet God

Bestselling Author John Ortberg

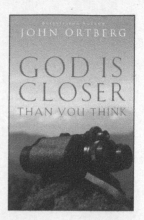

Intimacy with God can happen right now if you want it. A closeness you can feel, a goodness you can taste, a reality you can experience for yourself. That's what the Bible promises, so why settle for less? God is closer than you think, and connecting with him isn't for monks and ascetics. It's for business people, high school students, busy moms, single men, single women ... and most important, it's for YOU.

God Is Closer Than You Think shows how you can enjoy a vibrant, moment-by-moment relationship with your heavenly Father. Bestselling author John Ortberg reveals the face of God waiting to be discovered in the complex mosaic of your life. He shows you God's hand stretching toward you. And, with his gift for storytelling, Ortberg illustrates the ways you can reach toward God and complete the connection — to your joy and his.

Six-Session DVD Study also available.

Available in stores and online!

ZONDERVAN®
.com